Restored

in

Christ

Restored in Christ

SUSAN FARRUGIA

Restored in Christ
by Susan Farrugia

© Copyright 2019
SAINT PAUL PRESS, DALLAS, TEXAS

First Printing, 2019.

ISBN: 9781660250042

Printed in the U.S.A.

contents

introduction

Many have grown up with the idea that God is primarily a God of deprivation, a God of rules and regulations who needs to be appeased in order to love us, otherwise we bring His punishment and condemnation upon ourselves. God is love. This does not make of Him some sort of sweet sugary God, but rather because He does love us, He wants us to know His love, and in this love to walk with Him in the Truth. He wants us to be free from sin and the effects of sin which bind us up and make of us prisoners in the darkened cell of self. Our wrong understanding of who God is has created such a distortion; we either say He is all mercy and is never angry, which is not true, for that means there would be no justice, or else we see Him like a patriarchal tyrant God with the whip forever in His hands ready to come down on us should we falter. God is all mercy, ready to forgive us, for He calls us back to Himself. But

He is also just. He is holy, and sin and holiness are not compatible.

Because of this wrong image of God, it is no wonder one cannot see Him as Father, a true and loving Father who cares for all our needs and wants the very best for us. We have distorted the image of God the Father, and instead of turning to Him in love we have run away from Him in fear. Many of our earthly relationships have echoed this fear we have of God the Father in such a way that deep wounds, whether they are emotional, psychological, or spiritual wounds, they lie deeply embedded within our being. The Lord wants to heal us and restore us into the persons He has always meant us to be.

Healing does not happen automatically; it is not an instant coffee machine, but rather it comes as we courageously take that step forward, entering and resting in the presence of God. It is in His presence that all our pain can be released; the turbulence, our anguish, and even our anger can surface. It is in Him that we are able to forgive and slowly let go, step by step, of all that hinders and wounds us. It is then in listening to the Lord's affirming Word—His Word in Scripture—that we are made anew, restored one damaged emotion, one wound at a time. Allowing His Spirit and Word to touch us, our memories are healed and the negative words that once tore us apart can be uprooted. As His living, healing, and affirming

Word is spoken into us, spoken into our hearts, He "*makes all things new*" (Isaiah 43:18-19; Revelation 21:5).

In many ways, we can liken the Lord's work to that of an archaeologist. He is the Divine archaeologist who looks for and unearths the treasured artefact deeply embedded in the ruins of our pain and brokenness. Slowly, He cuts and chisels away at the surrounding rock, soil and stone. He removes the loose stones and very delicately brings up into daylight the once hidden artefact. Not wanting to damage the treasure held in His hands, He cleans the precious artefact with love and laborious dedication until finally all the soil, encrustations, and centuries of dirt is gone. He will delicately wash the artefact in a cleansing solution and dry it, placing it in the light for it to be seen and admired: a beautiful work of art, once lost but now found and restored to its original glory.

This is what the Father does with us. He calls us out from the ruins of our situations. He removes all the dirt we have accumulated in our lives through our sin, others' sin against us, all hurts and pain. He cleanses, heals, and purifies us with His blood and washes us clean until we are restored to the glory that is our true image in Christ.

As we travel down this road, and just as He came alongside the two disciples walking on the road to Emmaus after the Lord's Crucifixion and who had lost all hope and walked away from Jerusalem so despondent and dejected, the Lord comes alongside us and intervenes. He speaks to our heart, and asks us *"why are you so despondent?"* As His words enter into our hearts, we begin to feel His presence, and like those two disciples we can say, *"Did our hearts not burn within us when he spoke to us?"* Truly the Lord is here not only to listen to us but to heal, to touch the roots of our pains, to set us free from all that is enslaving us. This is salvation; it is the Truth that sets us free from the chains of the past as we cling to Him who is the Lord of all life.

He is the one who calls us by name. He knows who we are and knows how the mud and boulders of life have held us down. Slowly He calls us and tells us to 'rise up!' He has told us through the Prophet Isaiah:

> *But now thus says the LORD, he who created you, O Jacob, he who formed you, O Israel: "Fear not, for I have redeemed you; I have called you by name, you are mine. When you pass through the waters, I will be with you; and through the rivers, they shall not overwhelm you; when you walk through fire you shall not be burned, and the flame shall not consume you. For I am the LORD your God, the Holy One of Israel, your Saviour. I give Egypt as your ransom, Ethiopia and Seba in exchange for you. Because*

you are precious in my eyes, an• honoure•, an• I love you,
I give men in return for you, peoples in exchange for your
life. Fear not, for I am with you.

— Isaiah 43:1-5

The Father knows and calls us by name. He knows and calls you, yes, you, by name. As He whispers our name, your name, life bursts forth from His heart like torrents of living waters washing us and setting us free. Because He loves us, He gave us Jesus that we, through Him, in the power of the Holy Spirit will be set free and have eternal life beginning here on earth.

It is at the Lord's feet that we find life. We begin to know who He is, and in looking and gazing into His face, we then begin to understand who we are in HIM. It is only by looking at Him can our true selves become uncovered and find life.

It is a journey, a journey of love, and yes, many times painful, but a journey into life. Be encouraged and trust Him to do this in you . . . for He will accomplish all that He has started.

"I am sure that he who began a goo• work in you will bring it to completion at the •ay of Jesus Christ" (Philippians 1:6).

chapter one
our need for healing and restoration

In the transition that has been taking place in the Church, one of the major shifts has been between the relationship of the Church and the world. There has been a shift from the faith that had to be carefully guarded and kept safe from the contamination of the world to a faith that is lived out in the world, a faith that is continuously challenged to be strengthened, formed, and lived out in our contemporary and ordinary life. Many grew up in a world that was intact, everything was clearly defined especially the lines between good and evil. We now live in a world of less certainty with a lot of grey areas and where people are challenged to make decisions for themselves and think through their moral choices and commitments. This requires a well-formed conscience and an understanding of our faith. It requires most of all a relationship with Jesus Christ and a life lived in the Word of God.

In the course of this movement and change that was based on rules and regulations with an authority structure intact, morality was clearly defined in the 'dos and don'ts'. It is the Word of God that is the barometer of our lives. However, as years have gone by and in the name of progression, laws in countries, in the name of 'rights' have been enacted that have slashed and created deep wounds in the moral fibre not only of the countries but of people. With this gashing wound each person is launched into the sea of personal consciousness and is now open to a morality of conscience and personal responsibility. We have sadly lost the sense of sin and evil. Sin has been moved to the forum and discussion of psychology where valid psychological insights have been abused to the point of negating evil and sin. We have rationalised, intellectualised, blamed others, and found excuses beyond measure but have avoided the responsibility that is ours.

These insights have shown us that people are not totally free. We are all influenced by our upbringing, backgrounds, and circumstances. The human person is a complexity of different forces revealed in our behaviour. No matter how much we want to explain them away, we have come to a point where we cannot explain away evil or sin, so we deny its existence; we rationalise and cover each endeavour with the expression of personal right. It is as though these things do not exist! We have become so sophisticated that we naively think that evil does not exist or have relegated evil to the Middle Ages with the image of the devil sitting on our shoulder whispering into our ears as something out of a comic book.

This is exactly what the evil one wants us to believe and live. This leads us to a false assumption and naivete and we do not often take into account the very personal presence of evil, that everything is either good or bad, that someone has a psychological problem, or that sin does not exist. It fails to deal with the reality of evil within society. We lack the sense of our own sinfulness and our own capacity for evil giving us a false sense of security because we fail to appreciate the very real human struggle between choosing what is good, that is, what is of God, over evil and sin. This is what makes and forms the human person. This is the spiritual life.

Within us, there is a deep sense of loss; there is a sense of the loss of one's own worth and value which is at the heart of much spiritual death and loss of the true inner being. People may think that they do not have anything to give, are incapable of achieving anything worthwhile and so lose their sense of being all that God wants them to be. They live their lives on the superficial and meaningless level and fail to come to understand the reality of salvation, of the struggle between the choosing of good and of evil that is within us and around us; they feel helpless and powerless. As long as I am not doing anything truly bad then all is okay. However, the truth is, it is not alright. If I am not living in the light then I am in the dark and at best in the shadows but not in the light of Christ. There is a crisis of faith today because people fail to realise their need of Jesus Christ. There are none so blind as those who will not see.

Many times, because we fail to recognise evil for what it is, we can fall into a pseudo innocence, which is childishness. This is not being childlike as Christ would have us, but it is failing to understand the depths that are at work within the human person. Instead of dealing with the complexity of one's problems, the person HIDES behind his inability and weakness. We see this in many of the murder cases in the world at the moment. The person commits an atrocious murder, and the lawyers claim mental disability or sickness. That murder was evil. Yes, the man was mentally sick but not in a medical way. He was sick spiritually. Evil was the force at work, even on the psychological level, and man was its partner. This kind of attitude covers over evil and does not recognise it for what it is, so the right help cannot be given. Man needs to be healed, and it is Jesus Christ who heals and restores. All else are pointers and aides but do not heal. Theology, psychology, philosophy, sociology, etc., can only help; they are pointers and aides to many of the problems, but they cannot heal the problems. They do not restore dignity and wholeness to the human person. Christ does that.

Within the human person lies the cry for significance, the cry for acceptance and respect, the cry to be allowed to become and be oneself. It is three-dimensional: self-affirmation or self-esteem, self-assertion, and self-expression. For in self-expression, we reveal our inner self, and in so doing, we stand by what we believe. We affirm ourselves in our own right and our self-esteem grows. We are called to grow and form part of our community and society. The human person longs to be understood and listened to at his deepest level. We need to see what we do not see, hear what we do not hear, and speak what is to be feared if spoken. This lack of being, this inability to live through one's centre leaves the person lonely and frustrated;

there is no centre to grasp. Often it is not just anyone who must listen, for it could be that person in authority, that person whom we know means and understands something.

A person who is significant in one's life is the person who touches the deepest level of our existence, our feelings, convictions, hopes, and dreams. This cry of significance has taken many people down paths of destruction, but it is on that path that many have found Christ. It is in this need 'to become' that is so often disguised in the pursuit of power, money, drugs, alcohol, sex, materialism, the cult of the body, etc. It is the intensity to be recognised and accepted that find their expression in so many groups clamouring for attention. It is the attempt to fill the void inside instead of realising that the terrible spiritual void is one that only Christ can fill. There is the desperate need to discover and recognise our worth as human persons.

Yet, worth is also given; it is given and realised. It cannot be taken, for it is truly expressed by those who are important to us and we to them, those who hold us in their hearts. When received this way, we feel appreciated and are able to move forward, daring to discover its meaning in a deeper sense for ourselves. It is Christ alone and our surrender to Him. No one can take away another's loneliness, but we can walk with the other; only Christ can enter into that place and bring about a deep solitude that is found in and through listening prayer. When we enter into this place, we find ourselves as we should be: created in the image and likeness of God.

Man is meant and was created to be whole and holy. Wholeness and holiness, co-extensive and synonymous are meant to work in harmony with each other. Spiritual development and human growth go hand in hand in the development of a healthy human being. This does not mean that the person must be perfectly 'all together' psychologically to grow spiritually, nor does it mean that spiritual growth can ignore psychological factors in the development of the human person. However, it does mean that the integration of the two is the aim in the development of mature, healthy human beings.

chapter two
Christ in you, your Hope of Glory (Colossians 1:27)

Living and giving life

Jesus who is the Incarnate Word gives us life and through Him we enter into God's transcendent presence. He is God, the second Person of the Trinity, made man. The Letter to the Colossians speaks of Christ's pre-existence in eternity. It is in His indwelling of the Virgin Mary, through the power of the Holy Spirit that He who was eternal and one with the Father came into being, became the Incarnate One. This is so that we human beings—for He did not despise our mortality but became as one of us—might become unto Him. What is uncreated in symbolism becomes created for the transcendent is more real than what is on earth. Christ who is God made man, was the Incarnate one. When through baptism we receive the Holy Spirit, we have God alive and dwelling within. When God comes to live in us making of us temples of the Holy Spirit, we become indwelt. The indwelling of the Spirit within makes of God's life within me my Incarnational Reality[1]. It is God's presence with us and within us.

In the Holy Spirit given to us at baptism, we are called to share the life of Christ. In living incarnationally, we bring to light and truth that very presence of God, and through human beings God takes life in each person. Every baptised person is the temple of the Holy Spirit, and each unbaptised person is made in the image and likeness of God. How does God, the Eternal One, the Father, shines through us who are finite, the created, His creatures? It is in this aspect that I shall speak of giving life to what is dead or dying, broken or discarded within the human person.

What God the Father created to be whole and complete has been broken through sin whether it is our own personal sin or the sin of others against us. Because of this, the human

---

[1] Leanne Payne, Leanne Payne quoting C.S Lewis refers to the indwelling/abiding of Christ in the Christian as Incarnational Reality.

person has been defaced and wounded out of recognition of what the Father intended for him or her to be. Moreover, through wrong turnings, God's initial plans have gone awry and though redirection may be possible, for the Father always has a way to bring the person to complete wholeness in Him, the Father has created us to be 'persons'; we are to have 'being' in Him. To become persons, we have to enter into the journey and unfold the petals or layers of 'being and becoming' to find our true selves and be completed in Him. In Him, we become fully human and that is through His presence over and within us.

It is in Christ that we live and move and have our being. We begin to do His works and this does involve incarnation, an infilling of the Holy Spirit which we received at Baptism and at Confirmation to be reinforced and strengthened through prayer, the Sacraments, and living a life in the Spirit. In Christ, the will, intellect, imagination, feelings, and sensory being are blessed and hallowed and thus enlivened. We begin to live fully and to participate in the eternal. This is of the greatest importance, for as Christians, we must and should believe in Christ's real presence within us, not only in the Sacraments but incarnationally, working in and through us.

Sadly, modern man has lost the sense of the presence of God and to a great extent many Christians have failed to harness this understanding. This may be because of 'religious' teaching or because of a form of legalism of the whole Christian church. To enter into a lively presence of Christ is to live the Gospel and to uncover the treasure hidden therein. To give life is to bring fullness and help persons enter into that reality in the Spirit, to heal and to bring broken persons into wholeness in Christ.

Shattered and broken

Man and woman travel lonely roads where there are pitfalls and thieves, but the Gospel promises to the poor, the broken hearted, and those bound by sin and pride they will remain and be forever alive and new. We sail a ship that flounders through jagged rocks. Man needs to know that there is a Saviour who gives life and that life is given in abundance, freely. Man cannot walk his road or sail his ship alone; he needs the right winds to fill his sails. He needs the winds of the Spirit through faith that comes from an open and listening heart. He needs the faith of Mary, who as creature and mother, walks with us.

In giving life, the unseen is seen, the invisible is seen with the eyes of the heart and the inaudible with the ears of the heart. What is broken and shattered, like a very precious alabaster jar with all the contents strewn on the floor and trodden underfoot, Christ brings back together, piece by piece, to make whole. Creation is made new. *"I Am the Alpha and the Omega, I make all things new."* In giving life, we learn to love those around us and the world through us; we learn to collaborate with Christ; we do what we see Him do and He works in us. We can do nothing nor bear the right fruit on our own by our own endeavours, but we must do what the Son does who only does *"what he sees the Father doing, for whatever the Father does, the Son does likewise"* (John 5:19). Belief is no longer solely intellectual or doctrinal but is taken into every facet of our lives: the mind, intellect, the heart, and the senses. It is total and enveloping, overflowing to others. We, thus, become incarnational in Christ.

What has been discussed above has been given to us by Paul in his letter to the Ephesians:

"I pray that the God of our Lord Jesus Christ the Father of glory, may give you a spirit of wisdom and revelation as you come to know him, so that, with the eyes of your heart enlightened, you may know what is the hope to which he has called you, what are the riches of his glorious inheritance among the saints and what is the immeasurable greatness of his power for us who believe" (Ephesians 1:17-19).

Paul understood the importance of the Incarnation and the indwelling of Christ within him. He saturated his letters with this proclamation continuously underlying that it was Christ who was at work within him. *"It is not I who lives but Christ who lives in me"* (Galatians 2:20); this mystery given to us is *"Christ in you, your hope of glory"* (Colossians 1:27). John, in his letter, speaks of this Incarnate indwelling: *"Greater is he who is in me than he who is in the world"* (1 John 4:4). This indwelling is safeguarded through the continuous 'abiding' in Christ (John 15:5), for without Him we can do nothing nor will our fruit last (John 15:8). This understanding that to be in Christ and to be 'indwelt' by Christ was essential to the early Christians and should be and must be essential to the true Christian today.

I would like to quote a favourite Christian author, C.S. Lewis, an intense Oxford Literary scholar and figure in Christian Apologetics. In speaking about Incarnational Reality, Lewis says in his book *Mere Christianity,*

> *When Christians say the Christ-life is in them, they do not mean simply something mental or moral. When they speak of being 'in Christ' or of Christ being 'in them' this is not simply a way of saying that they are thinking about Christ or copying Him. They mean that Christ is actually operating through them; that the whole mass of Christians*

are the physical organism through which Christ acts - that

we are his fingers an• muscles, the cells of His bo•y.[2]

Since Christians form a mystical unity with one another through their fellowship and are incorporated into Christ (1 Corinthians 10:17) the belief and living out of this reality, the Real Presence amongst us must be a tangible means of life and healing. This was most evident in the early Christians, for how would a three-months stay of St. Paul in Malta (Acts 28) explain such a drastic transformation of a population from pagan deities to Christ. The rites of Baptism and the Lord's Supper were understood as special means by which God's grace was revealed and received, by which His Spirit was mediated to man. This is the same Spirit that provides the unity, who indwells and gifts the believer mediating forgiveness and strength.

---

[2] C. S. LEWIS, *Mere Christianity*, Glasgow, 2001, 36.

chapter three
reconciliation
is restoration

The Christian view is one of man, the creature, fully reconciled to God the creator. To be reconciled in every aspect is to be healed, restored, forgiven, and loved, and this is to know the 'Good' of God. Separation from oneself is separation from God, and this is brokenness and negative. God does not want separation from self for that separated self is cut off from the light of God and left in darkness. To be fully incarnational is to be fully restored and reconciled in Christ. When speaking of reconciliation, one would automatically understand it to mean forgiveness, but this is only a one-sided facet. Reconciliation is the full restoration of the self, the full part of the self that is loved and thus becomes and is called and restored into being.

This is salvation. To be loved is salvation. Love makes whole and heals. It is through Christ's command that the empowering to heal comes. Christ has empowered His followers and disciples to heal because He knows that all men in their inner beings have broken relationships and are separated from self. For man to regain wholeness in every aspect of his life, the relationship between himself and God, himself and 'man' meaning others, himself and nature, and within his innermost being must be healed. This healing must include the will, the unconscious mind and heart, the emotions, and the intuitive and imaginative faculties.

The key to this healing is Incarnational Reality, being filled with God's Spirit, and seeking to dwell in His presence. It is to choose union and communion with God. As we enter and live in the presence of God, we are conscientiously choosing His presence rather than separateness which, in effect, is living out of the 'old man' the Adamic self. To choose life is to choose integration of self instead of disintegration or separation. It is to choose love in the Trinity and to enter into relationship with God, others, creation, and, ultimately, with self. It is knowing and being, for the Father is continuously 'singing' us into being in Christ. The Father is always at work. To enter into this, one needs to be 'poor in spirit' for only in the knowledge of one's poverty can one hope to cling to Christ's richness and fullness of life.

In union with Christ is to live, *"For we are what he has ma●e us, create● in Christ Jesus for goo● works, which Go● prepare● beforehan● to be our way of life"* (Ephesians 2:10). To live this life is to live in the 'higher self,' the true 'I.' It is in this sense that 'I become' and thus 'I AM.' For being loved by God in and through others and loving others gives life, and we become and are called into being.

God the Father calls us into being in Christ and in so doing delights in us, His children and creation, as an artist would delight in his masterpiece. We are the Father's masterpiece, the work and fruit of His love, the creation of His hands. Thus, to be held and loved by the Father is life-giving and works its way into our existence and onto others and those whom we meet, thus turning even our sufferings into wounds of life for others.

Restoration is healing

In the command to heal, Christ asks for the restoration of the essence of man—the whole person—for in our brokenness we have cut ourselves off from the very source of life. This condition envelops us like masks, and like Adam and Eve we hide from the presence of God. The real 'I' lies buried under deep layers of the false self, behind masks, and must be given life. The arid ground, our revealed self-baked layers through exposure to the elements covers the true inner self, the core of who we are and our real being. The desert hardens forming a crust that covers the underground living waters that try to surge to the surface. It is love. It is the prophetical Word spoken and proclaimed to that ground that cracks open and makes fissures in the hard sand allowing the true self to gush through in a surge of life-giving water. Christ came to free man from the bondage of the false self and to remove the masks. This is clearly seen in John chapter 4 with the Samaritan woman. This is the Good News.

The Lord wants to heal the whole person emotionally, psychologically, physically, sociologically, and spiritually. All that makes the human person as ordained by God to live amongst people and to be fully accepted and acceptable. Broken people mean a broken society. When insecurity and fears cloud a person's life it affects the community and, hence, society. When people are healed, the community is healed, and society is healed. The Lord comes to heal not only the human person, bringing reconciliation within each person individually, but this healing also pours out into the community. There is restoration with one's neighbour because there is restoration within.

This is what the disciple is called to do. He, too, is to be healed and given life as he is to give life in turn. As Christ, anointed in His baptism in the Spirit, walked the roads of Israel to free man from the hell of self-will and pride, from the pain of physical sickness and deaths, so are we commanded to do the same: to proclaim the liberty of captives and freedom to prisoners (Luke 4:18-19). It is to call forth in Jesus' name the real person, the healed person. Every door of our being is to be opened to the Redeemer who stands at the door and knocks that He may come in and eat with us (Revelation 3:20). It is then that we are healed in spirit, in intellect and will, in our intuitive, imaginative and sensory faculties, and physically.

To bring Christ into the lives of others is to be a channel of Christ's love. To love is to heal and to heal is to love. Christ's aim is to saturate the life of the believer with His presence. This is what conversion and transformation are. This was Paul's transformation. It is an ongoing process of being filled with Christ. The Holy Spirit truly present and operative in the human spirit, in the human person, is capable of resurrecting every faculty of man. It is from this healing presence that the flowing waters of life, those underground waters that flow of the Spirit, give life and have the power to heal, restoring the Adam within us and creating us anew.

Fallen but redeemed

The unfallen Adam and Eve could hear and walk with God. They could listen to Him. They had union with Him. They were God-conscious and not self-conscious. They were not forever looking over their shoulders and wondering what the other was saying or thinking. They were uncluttered and free. Their eyes could see clearly because their hearts and minds were singular. They had that one face that could look up at the sound of the voice of God and look into His face. They could look into and touch the face of God. Their spirits were alive and they had authority over nature including themselves. Their faculties were under the control of the Spirit which was indwelt by God. Their faculties were in accord with God and with nature. Their consciences were clear, and they certainly did not have that bad self-image that is so prevalent today.

Their mind was not cluttered with false ideologies nor were they repressed or suppressed. Adam was not a threat to Eve nor was Eve a threat to Adam. There was no rejection of self or the other. They were in 'being'; their personhood was contained, held, and formed. They had received only love and love made them whole. Theirs was the relationship of love, and, in turn, they were channels of love to all creation calling each creature by name thus exerting authority over creation that was entrusted to them. They were stewards of God's creation. In their unfallen state, they were blessed, and they blessed all and everything around them, experiencing the true and real presence of God. They did not know separation from God.

Evil brought darkness and separation. This now happens to Adam and Eve, and in their fall, the strike came like a knife cutting through their very being bringing separation. The knife cut through their relationship with each other and with creation and ultimately with God. They lost the presence and voice of God. They lost His face, and the 'I' within them fell into that deep abyss of pain and rejection. Adam and Eve had to live out of the 'false self.' They had to live separated from self and from each other. Man and woman were a threat to each other and the masks had to be worn. Pain entered and light and truth gave way to lies and darkness.

chapter four
to be made
whole in Christ

This separation found in man, the separation of self needs to become one before man can know who he is. We need to know our identity, and for the Christian, it is imperative that he knows and lives out of his or her identity as a son or daughter of the Father. There is the need to obey the Word, the Rhema word, the Word that is alive and active. Christ is the living Word, the Logos and calls us to enter into His Word (rhema) for *"man does not live by bread alone but by every Word that comes out of the mouth of God"* (Matthew 4:4).

This is what it means to become perfect. Perfection does not begin with moral order but in the essence of being that works itself out into moral order. It is then through being, and this being is now in Christ, that I can do the works of Christ and live as Christ would have me live. In truth, we are in a continuous movement of 'becoming,' of 'transformation' until we reach the fullness of who we are to be, full personhood, and that is achieved only in Heaven where we will see the Father, where we will see Christ face to face and know fully as we are known.

Helping others to enter into this essence of being is calling persons into obedience that is life-giving. The Word speaks to us and we are called and we respond. This is obedience, and thus, we enter into the freedom of the Word and integrated in self. Christ on the Cross restored the self and in giving His 'I,' the Incarnate One took upon Himself all of Adam, and in giving up Himself restored and brought out of the abyss Adam's lost self. Christ's restoration of Adam's dignity brought life in such a transformed manner that the new creation is now greater than the first for it is achieved by the Blood of the Incarnate One.

In giving life, this is the life that is to be lived, a life worth living for. Through experience of the living presence of God, Christ reconciling man to Himself, to the Father, and to the created world, Christ reconciles man with his true self; he finds his 'I,' his true sense of being. In doing so, the 'I' can then relate to others and bring forth others. This is true Christianity: the giving of life to each; Christ within each one calling forth the other into life and being.

A new creation

As Christians, we have lost much in our understanding of fullness in Christ, and this needs restoration. In finding our identity in Christ, we no longer seek it in a role, in a career or profession. We are not determined or defined by fears of failures or by what others think. This is the justification that we have been called to; it is justification in Christ alone. This gives freedom from what others might think or judge, freedom to do what is right and the freedom to be; it is freedom to love and beyond. The Law restricts, but the Spirit and truth gives freedom. Fear no longer conditions the inner life nor do the circumstances outside, but the person is enabled to confront and to deal with these situations rather than be shaped or broken by them. The Christian listens attentively to the Spirit and what is paradoxically seen as to have lost itself, the person truly finds himself and for the first time 'lives.'

This creativity springs forth from God in us, the springs that gush from underground to give life to what is seen as the desert. This is the work of God alone. This is not done by man, and all man must do is to collaborate with God and let God work. Christ in man resurrects the whole of man and releases him from the chaos within all his faculties. It is to the whole man that the living Jesus relates and not the soul alone or the spirit alone as though his sensory faculties and emotions were not part of him. It is then the whole person must collaborate with Jesus and involve himself in his 'becoming,' in his 'transformation.' This is Christ's initiative and his work in the person. We enter into union and communion with the God who is creator and who is re-creating us, and in so doing, we become all that we are meant and were meant to be. Love can then flow from the uncreated into the created and then to others. For we must all become a channel of this love to others. It is by virtue of love flowing through us that we begin to bless and to name our brothers and sisters, calling forth the real 'I,' the true person forth and to enter into the depths of the other as Christ would have it.

The true person found, therefore, in the understanding of what is held deeply within, the life of Christ, is expressed in the person as giving life and celebrating life. The Incarnational Reality is expressed in the giving of life in another and receiving life from the other. It is living in the 'I – thou' relationship. To be in touch with our deepest being, Christ

Incarnate within requires prayer—listening prayer. It comes from that sense of being that is found in Christ who speaks into our deepest core calling us forth and calling us into life. Our deepest being is held within Him who is the source of life and being. He gives us space and time to grow.

Having said the above, this is what is required to bring life into what would otherwise seem a mundane and mediocre Christianity that seems to be alive but is dead and lukewarm, to be spat out of God's mouth (Revelation 3:14-22). It is not wrapping ourselves in a moral straitjacket or external religious observances that mean nothing when in the heart of man there is nothing but hardness of heart and arid ground *"because these people ⟨r⟩aw near with their mouth an⟨d⟩ honour me with their lips, while their hearts are far from me an⟨d⟩ their worship of me is a human comman⟨d⟩ment learne⟨d⟩ by rot"* (Isaiah 29:13). These are works, externalism, that may in truth benefit the receiver in terms of charity, but do nothing for the giver.

There is to be cohesion within the person and that person's action for it to bear true fruit. This is not life but dead actions. There is the need for transformation, to enter into the Word and be enlivened by it; to enter into a living understanding of who we are in Christ and receive our identity from Him. Then, and only then will the external take its proper and rightful place without pomp or fuss. We will worship in Spirit and in Truth for the light of truth will be within us and the Spirit will guide us as it guides the Church. But let us never forget that each baptised person forms the Church. We are the Church, the holy priesthood of Christ, the family of God redeemed by the Blood of Christ that cries out louder than the blood of Abel. This is our inheritance. This is who we are and who we are called to be.

There are many who have gone before us, who in their own way have sought the truth within themselves and outside of themselves. The Light of God is forever present in whatever age or era, guiding and teaching. This saving history has carried the human person forward from his or her genesis into the present moment. Woman and man are not without turmoil and falls. Both are good, created as good by God the Father. Both have fallen in their nature but have been redeemed through Christ. If as a body, as a Church, we do not harness this depth of truth, a truth that is not just defined as doctrinal but an experienced truth, the truth of our Incarnational Reality, we risk the tragedy of being lost in a maze of externalisms and will never find the self, the truth of the self, of our personhood in Christ. Christ is within each of us; we are 'indwelt' by God and that should be enough to set us thinking, to reflect this awesome wonder that God lives and is alive and at work within each and everyone one of us. This is the true celebration of life. This is our Incarnational Reality.

chapter five
listening prayer

"Be Still and Know that I am God" (Psalm 46:10).

We, as persons, can only receive our truest healing as we listen to the Lord and discern His Word upon our life and actions in His light. To listen to God in prayer is to look up to Him with intuitive thinking. It is through the eyes and ears of the heart that we see and hear God. Through it we apprehend the transcendent, that which is beyond the physical or material. Listening prayer is in effect a feminine attribute of the human person. Quoting C.S. Lewis' famous quote *"in relation to God we are all female."*[3] Taken from his book *Till we have Faces,* this

---

[3] Clive Staple Lewis – *Till we have Faces.*

quote echoes Ephesians 5:25-27 in that as Church, we are all the Bride of Christ.

The Scriptures are full of examples of people who listened to God and responded. The Word of God is the inspired Word through which God also speaks. The Word of God is alive and active, discerning the thoughts of man. It is the double-edged sword cutting through bone and marrow "*for man does not live by bread alone but by every Word that comes out of the mouth of God*" (Matthew 4:4). Listening to the Word in Scripture and within our hearts bring us into intimate union with Christ. By virtue of our Baptism we have the indwelling of the Holy Spirit who alone knows the depths of God and knows us in our deepest being. When we pray, when we listen, and when we respond we do so through the power of the Holy Spirit who helps us in our weakness.

He is the one who brings to remembrance words and actions. He is the one who enlightens the mind and opens our heart to the mind and heart of Christ. Man is indwelt. Christ abides in us and we in Him. He is nearer to us than we are to ourselves. In union with Christ, the whole of our being is made holy. We are not divided but one, Incarnate. The body is not to be despised, nor our hearts or minds, nor are we to be perceived as a mere 'container' for the Holy Spirit, for that is a Platonic understanding. We are the temple of the Holy Spirit.

All that God has created is GOOD. We are made in God's image and likeness.

Jesus who does not disdain our bodies took the likeness of our body showing us its holiness and goodness. We are made in the image of Christ Incarnate before Jesus was made man, that is, when He was conceived and born. Each human person is made in this image of God, of Jesus made man, and each person is unique and uniquely loved. Each person has his own unique relationship with God, and God knows how to reach and speak to each person according to that person's character and personality. In listening prayer, we mature as Christians, we are healed and restored, and it is a walk in the Spirit, no matter the depths of our weaknesses, needs, or brokenness.

True listening is obedient listening. To listen to God is to obey Him. This listening and responding prayer calls out the real 'I' in each one of us, and it is from this real 'I' that the true self is called forth to live. The love that is God calls us forth and this love flows from the uncreated to the created giving life. He who is the 'I AM' calls each and every one of us forth from the tomb of the old self into the light of our new created being. This is achieved as we listen to the voice deep within and in Scripture. This reality is found primarily in the person of Jesus Christ who gives us our redemption. Truth is spoken deep within, and it is the response of faith that opens the doors to our healing as we listen to the Spirit's healing word and prompting. This is the message of love flowing down to us and taking us up into it. This is the message of the Cross, where the great reversal of the Fall began. At the Cross love and life were given freely to all mankind and creation, and from there life began and death would have no more hold.

Christ who is Himself the Word and Truth brings those of us who are *in Him* to the place of ultimate healing communion with the Father. There can be no dialogue without listening prayer. Without Scripture, without listening, we become like a dried twig or hard ground unable to grow any fruit or become all that we are meant to be. In Christ, we are taken to the Father and as we hear Him, we come to our *Full Identity,* we know who we are and who we were created to be and become. We pass from immaturity to maturity. When we live in the presence of God, we learn to acknowledge always the God who is really there; we pray continually as the Scriptures exhort us to do (1 Thessalonians 5:17).

When we do this, we are opened to receive the Word He always speaks. We enter a path of listening obedience we would not find through striving (that is through the Law), a path of freedom where we joyfully realize and acknowledge

Jesus as Lord and carry out His will. To acknowledge the reality that is unseen requires great effort of our will at first and we need to learn to be disciplined in prayer and the practice of the Presence. In this listening, we come out of our spiritual adolescence, our immaturity and begin to mature in Christ. To listen to God is to receive wisdom from above and like Jesus we grow as we continually receive it.

Listening prayer is a vital facet of God's presence with us. It is a place of freedom from the voices of the world, the flesh, and the devil. Those latter voices when listened to and obeyed pull us toward non-being and death. To fail to listen to God is to be listening to one or another or all of those voices. It is to miss the vital walk in the Spirit and our immensely creative collaboration with Him to become the new self, one in union with Him and maturing in Him.

Listening also brings us into covenant relationship with God for when someone declared Mary blessed for being the mother of Jesus, He replied, *"Blesse⸱ rather are those who hear the Wor⸱ of Go⸱ an⸱ keep it"* (Luke 11:27-28). Jesus refers to the deeper meaning of listening to the Spirit which is a sign of entering into covenant relationship. When the Word is spoken to us, we are to safeguard the Word which brings in us life, not only eternal life but the healing Word that makes us whole and that leads to the fullness of life. This makes us more and more children of the Father as the Word of God conforms within us, re-creating us anew. In the listening, we can also enter into suffering. When the Lord heals there is often suffering, but He compares this to a woman in labour about to give birth to the child. After the pain there will be joy; there will be the resurrection from the sorrow: *"so you have sorrow now but I will see you again an￼ your hearts will rejoice an￼ no one will take that joy from you"* (John 16:22-23).

A hindrance to listening prayer is when the head and heart are split; we are separated from our own hearts; we deny parts of our own soul as valid. This is also true when we also place the mind above the heart instead of holding them in balance. We can understand God in a limited way intellectually, but it is the heart that intuits the transcendent. We need both heart and mind to be open to the infiniteness of God, to the heart and mind of God. The philosophers of the Enlightenment tried to rationalize God only to end up denying the existence of the Incarnation and the transcendence of God within man.

You are invited to listen to the Word of God and to take heed to what He is saying to you deep in your heart and mind. Do not let the Word fall away and be trodden upon, but taste the Word and allow the Lord to bring you the healing He intends for you.

chapter six

the great exchange – the cross and salvation

"But God shows his love for us in that while we were yet sinners Christ died for us" (Romans 5:8).

Many times, we as Christians can have a wrong understanding of the Cross.

This comes from the wrong image we have of God the Father and the depth of the meaning of forgiveness.

How many times have we heard, read, or even prayed the text John 3:16:

"For God so loved the world that he gave his only Son, that whoever believes in him should not perish but have eternal life."

As we look to Christ and the Cross, the truth that Jesus came to take away our sins takes on a definite place in our hearts and minds. But it is not just our sins but the consequences and effects of sin.

What is the truth of the Passion and Cross of our Lord Jesus Christ?

It is what we can call "The Great Exchange." Jesus took on our sins and became sin so that we can be free. No amount of striving, no amount of our struggle to obey the laws of God can take away our sins or purify us from sin. It is Jesus' sacrifice, the Paschal lamb who takes away the sins of the world. His blood alone can set us free. Our love and obedience are a response to that sacrifice, not a means to gain salvation; we cannot do it. We cannot attain our own salvation, for it is a free gift of the Father through Jesus Christ. What we need to do is to receive it.

When we say that Jesus paid for it all with His Blood, are we to understand that God the Father is a God who *emands* that someone pay the price of the sins of man like some sort of banker? Do we see the Father like someone we owed and we could not pay back so the Father took this payment or punishment from Jesus? First Peter 1:18 says: *"You know that you were ransomed from the futile ways inherited from your fathers, not with perishable things such as silver or gol♦, but with the precious bloo♦ of Christ."*

As we allow the eyes and heart of the Father, in the Spirit, to lead us deeper into the meaning of the Cross of His beloved Son Jesus and its work of salvation, we open our hearts that we may be saved by the Truth.

God made us in His image and likeness—beautifully and wonderfully made. Yet through deceit, Adam and Eve believed the lies of the evil one and fell into sin. To this very day man still believes the deceit and lies of the evil one. The evil one has the world in its tight grasp. What does the Father do? He knows that man is unable to save himself, to struggle out of the pit, to come out of the grasp of the evil one, out of the trap he has fallen into, no matter what he does. So, He promises to send one born of a woman who would save us. For in this alone can the purity and holiness of God redeem the sinfulness of man. Man cannot attain salvation for himself for he is now fallen and sinful. The Holy One, the Incarnate One alone can do this. This is the ransom/redemption. Did the Father want to exact His payment/retribution/payback? No. He wanted to save us. So, the Son came as one of us, a human being, like us in all things but without sin (Philippians 1:6-11). He is God and also Man, the Incarnate One. The evil of the world had its way with Him. He allowed it to be so (Jesus was always in control) for that was the only way. He willed it to happen, so He allowed Himself to be taken captive and to be crucified instead of us.

The evil one thought '*Right, now I will have them all – the Son an• the human person.*' Little did he know that evil cannot hold Him who is without sin. Because Jesus was without sin, unlike Adam and Eve and unlike us, He was able to carry the burden of the chains of sin and death on the Cross. Christ took all sin and the effects of sin upon Himself. He took our death, which is the final effect and culmination of sin, and because He is the sinless one, death could not hold Him. Jesus broke through the chains of sin and death and rose from the dead. All the effects of sin upon mankind and the final boundary of death had been broken. They would no longer hold us in bondage. The evil one was defeated. He is a defeated enemy. His plans are defeated, his power is defeated, his stranglehold is defeated but only if we walk in the Lord and in the power and truth of the Cross and Resurrection. We have been saved and baptised into the Cross and Resurrection of Jesus Christ. We are saved and children of the Kingdom, but we must also, with the Lord, work out our freedom one day at a time. Paul tells us "*work out your own salvation with fear an• trembling*"; for it has been won for us by the Cross of Christ.

You will surely say but evil is still in the world. Yes, most definitely, but that is because men prefer to live in the darkness of evil than in the light of Holy Truth. We have choices and the choices we make determine our eternal life. However, though the evil one has been defeated he still runs around like a lion waiting to devour us. We are still in an almighty battle. He is like a large dragon swinging and lashing his tail furtively. Though he is still around, we must remember that he is a defeated enemy and *"we are more than conquerors through him who loves us"* (Romans 8:37).

> *What then shall we say to this? If God is for us, who is against us? He who did not spare his own Son but gave him up for us all, will he not also give us all things with him? Who shall bring any charge against God's elect? It is God who justifies; who is to condemn? Is it Christ Jesus, who died, yes, who was raised from the dead, who is at the right hand of God, who indeed intercedes for us? Who shall separate us from the love of Christ? Shall tribulation, or distress, or persecution, or famine, or nakedness, or peril, or sword? As it is written; "For thy sake we are being killed all the day long; we are regarded as sheep to be slaughtered." No, in all these things we are more than conquerors through him who loves us. For I am sure that*

neither ♦eath, nor life, nor angels, nor principalities, nor
things present, nor things to come, nor powers, nor height,
nor ♦epth, nor anything else in all creation, will be able to
separate us from the love of Go♦ in Christ Jesus our Lor♦.

— Romans 8:31-39

What is happening when we say that Jesus takes away all sins? It is not just the sins we commit, the sins we confess, but the sins against us, all the effects of our sins which means the shame, guilt, brokenness, and all that comes with the fallen attributes of the human person (an alcoholic father or mother, a broken family, divorce, abortion, domination, etc.). He has paid for it all with His Blood, and He wants to heal the effects of that sin and its consequences to bring restoration and new life, a new beginning. However, this is not a magical situation. Jesus waits for us to bring our sin, our brokenness, our weaknesses to Him. We do need to repent of any wrong doing. We need conversion, a *metanoia*. Jesus does not just take them (our sins) but wants us to work with Him, co-operate with Him. He looks deeply into our hearts, shows us our situation, and asks us to give them to Him. In listening prayer, we learn and see that which is beyond the material. We see into the transcendence of truth. We see things exactly as they are. In His love, we can see the truth for what it is, come out of our denial, and look unto Him, giving Him all that is burdening us. There is no condemnation in any of this, but salvation, only loving conviction of the Holy Spirit. Condemnation does not come from the Lord, but from the evil one who accuses the people of God day and night (Revelation 12:10).

The Father allowed the sin of the world to go its full length when they crucified Christ. Jesus was obedient to the end. He cried in the Garden to the Father to save Him from this hour. But His food was to do the will of the Father. Where Adam and Eve had failed, where you and I fail, Jesus was to drink the cup to the bitter end. When He drank the cup, His thoughts were on you and on me. The Father encouraged Him and was with Him.

It was dark and the storm clouds of evil were all around Jesus. The Father saw His beloved Son, His body torn to shreds, His mind at breaking point, His breath gasping. *"Truly this was the Son of Go·"* (Matthew 27:54; Mark 15:39), the Centurion said. The Father looked upon His Son and when He saw Him, He also saw you and me. It is we who should have been crucified in His place for our sins, but they crucified the sinless one instead. When Jesus hung on the Cross for those three hours all the sin of mankind, past, present, and future clung to Him. The Father who is ALL HOLY, ALL LOVE looked upon

His Son, and when He saw the sin that stuck to His Son, He turned His face away from His Son and darkness covered the earth. Holiness and sin cannot and will never be compatible. The eternal abyss that is sin, its consequences and effects in and on the human person was lived out in Jesus. Jesus entered into that abyss to break the chains that bind us to the strongholds of all sin, its effects, and its consequences. Jesus felt the separation that comes from the worst possible sin that man can do or conceive, the sin of despair, indifference, disdain, unforgiveness, and hate.

"Eli, Eli, lema Sabachthani – my God, my God, why have your forsaken me?" (Psalm 22:2; Matthew 27:46). Sin separates us from the Father, from God; that is its consequence: Separation from the holy One. But Jesus came to bring us back to the Father and to give us new life, hope, and a future (Jeremiah 29:11).

Suffering

All suffering is wrong for it is not only a result of sin but is a mystery in itself. Suffering is not in God's plan but we can change suffering around through the Cross of Christ. Suffering hurts the heart of the Father for it is the fruit of sin and the Father experiences great sorrow over sin. Do we sorrow over our sin and those of others and the world?

Godly and worldly sorrow

There is a great difference between Godly sorrow and worldly sorrow over sin and selfishness. Paul, in 2 Corinthians 7:9-10, tells us that *"Go•ly grief pro•uces repentance that lea•s to salvation an• brings no regret, but worl•ly grief pro•uces •eath."* Repentance is not just being sorry; it is being sorry enough to stop doing wrong. Godly sorrow is not just the confession of sin, nor is it feeling bad about something we may have done. It is a *metanoia;* it brings conversion. Godly sorrow understands how sin hurts God, ourselves, and others. It produces change within us. We hate sin but love goodness. When we love God, then obeying His commandments come naturally. We do not try to obey God to get to Heaven or to avoid hell, to be respected or to get something from God (I was good so I deserve a pat on the back!). That is a gift/reward attitude and is a very superficial attitude of the spiritual life. We obey Him because He loves us and we are called to respond to that love. We all sin. There is not one of us who has not sinned for as 1 John 1:8-10 says:

"If we say we have no sin, we •eceive ourselves, an• the truth is not in us. If we confess our sins, he is faithful an• just, an• will forgive our sins an• cleanse us from all unrighteousness. If we say we have not sinne•, we make him a liar, an• his wor• is not in us."

God's heart is broken by pride, hatred, bitterness, dishonesty, greed, and all forms of selfishness, but the opposite also pleases His heart. We need to let our sin, our anger turn to grief over our sin. Anger only makes us more bitter, but Godly sorrow brings us the Lord's healing.

The Father's heart is broken over our sin for it wounds us terribly. Though we know He is merciful we cannot presume on His mercy and kindness or just take the Lord for granted. We can depend on it but never abuse it. As parents who love their children, we know that our children know what is wrong and what is right. They do not take things for granted, but they most definitely try us. As parents, we should not be indifferent to the wrong they have done, but correct it firmly yet lovingly. When we do not acknowledge our sin, that blocks us from receiving the love of the Father which is always there for us. We are not free to receive or enjoy the Father's love and acceptance. We feel we need to constantly do things to receive it.

Even if others wrong us and we react and likewise do wrong, that does not excuse us. We must deal with our own attitudes and actions, accepting responsibility for what we have done, said, or thought, and ask the Father's forgiveness for that.

There is no sin or brokenness which cannot be redeemed or restored. One has to only go to Jesus. It may be a long journey for many, a journey of repentance, restoration, healing, and making new. The Lord delivers us from the clutches and strongholds of evil to bring us into the kingdom of His love and light.

Jesus had told Philip *"The Father an● I are one – if you have seen me you have seen the Father"* (John 14:9). What was the Father's heart at that moment of Jesus' death? It was being wrenched, and I believe that the earth could not hold the pain of the Father's heart for the earth shuddered and quaked and was covered in darkness as the Father saw His Son die with the weight of all sin and the effects of sin upon Him. As Jesus died on the Cross He cried out, *"My Go● my Go●, Why have you forsaken me – Eli, Eli, lema Sabachthani."* Then *"It is finishe●; into your han●s I commen● my Spirit."*

The work of Satan was broken. The stranglehold Satan had on man was defeated. In that moment man was taken into the depths, his chains broken, Adam cried out, 'My Saviour lives!' First John 3:8 tells us *"The reason the Son of Go● appeare● was to ●estroy the works of the ●evil."* The evil one had held mankind in the bondage of deceit, disobedience, and sin. Through His Passion and Cross, Jesus did His redemptive work, and now the Great Exchange must take place. The work of the Cross is eternal. There is no time set upon it. Though historically it happened 2,000 years ago, it is still alive whenever we pray and call upon the One who was slain. At every Mass, we relive it through the Eucharist as though it was happening then; it is a perpetual memorial.

Many times, we feel like Jesus in the Garden of Gethsemane when we cannot walk any further. People we have trusted have let us down or even betrayed us. The Lord's suffering and struggle in the Garden cover us. Whenever we suffer, are sick physically, emotionally, physiologically, etc., we go to the necessary doctor. His Cross heals us. *"He took our sicknesses upon him, he was stricken by grief"* (Isaiah 53:3-7).

Jesus had His clothes ripped from Him. He was naked and derided. How many times have we been stripped of our dignity? Stripped from what was rightfully ours? The evil one is trying to steal our inheritance freely given to us by the Father. The pain is unbearable, yet by His own shame we are healed.

They whipped Jesus with the flagellum. This is a Roman tool for scourging. It is a leather thong with iron ends. Though Scripture does not say how many times He was scourged, it does inform us that it was Paul who was given the forty lashes minus one (2 Corinthians 11:24) which was the punishment given by Jewish law (Deuteronomy 25:3). Every lash upon

Jesus' body are the lashes we receive when people wound us with their actions and abuse. We feel like death as the agony covers us. But by His stripes we are healed (Isaiah 53:4-6). They placed a cloak upon Him, a rod in His hand, and a crown of thorns upon His head in mockery.

The crown of thorns that pierced His head heals our depressions; it heals our mental sicknesses. His emotional pain and psychological suffering heal our own emotions and psychological pains and disorders. The mockery He received heals us from the wounds of the tongue of others, their scorn and verbal abuse and from our own sinful tongues. He is subjugated to the jeering crowd. How many times do people say things against us and we are unable to defend ourselves, or know that what we say would be useless, so we stay silent even as Jesus did? His silence is our saving grace. Whatever Jesus suffered, He suffered that we might be freed and healed. On the Cross of Christ, we place all our sin, sicknesses, brokenness, and failings for the Lord to take unto Himself.

This is all the Great Exchange.

Man is fallen and we know this, but after the original fall and sin, man spiraled into sin and the effects of sin culminated upon us. Generation upon generation. Sin, its consequences and effects come to a stop when faced with the Cross of Christ with a deep and sincere heart. It is only the Cross of Christ that can take away the sin and cleanse and heal us from the effects.

In the Gospels, Jesus healed continuously, not only physically, but also the pain and suffering of rejection and so many psychological situations. He is the great physician and psychologist.

We bring all of our suffering to Christ's Passion and Cross. We give them to Him and receive life, healing, and restoration in exchange. We give Him death, the death deep within so that He breathes His life into us. Our physical death, the last frontier of man is the wages we must pay for our sins. Death has been won, for death has been conquered in life. Death could not hold Jesus down and He rose on the third day. This, too, is our resurrection in every single situation we overcome, for *"We are more than conquerors through Him who love us"* (Romans 8:37). In Christ Jesus, we rise to new life. In each area where there is darkness His Cross brings life and the light of truth.

Jesus won over all sin and its consequences and effects – what we must do is believe, claim and live this Great Divine Exchange, a term penned by the late Derek Prince – when all things are made new.

Yet, what of forgiveness? The Father forgives us our sins in Christ Jesus who gave up His life for us. We, too, are to forgive others their trespasses against us. Are we ready to forgive or do we make excuses? Are we ready to accept the forgiveness of others or are we too proud to do so? Do we bring our spiritual brokenness to the Lord and ask Him to forgive us? He does so immediately for He loves a repentant heart and restores that heart to health.

From Jesus' wounds love flows that fills us: the blood from His hands and feet; the pierced wound on His side from which flows the living stream of life His blood and water. This is the Spirit and healing life. We stand under this fountain of life, being washed down, cleansed, and healed.

The Father's heart is broken over sin. If we allow our hearts to be touched by the pain of the Father over things that break His heart, then He will be at the centre of our lives, and, yes, at least we can start in Him to put our own world back together again.

The prayer

Lord, You became that fool for me, disfigured and despised, for Your loving heart could not bear to see my iniquity. My sin took me further and further away from You until there was no light to see. In my brokenness, I was like a shattered vase. Who could put me together again? Yet your work is perfect. Into that darkness You came, so meek and so humble. You touched the ugliness of sin and the stings of my shame and took it upon Yourself. You soothed my pain and breathed Your life into me and bade me live again. Your love could not bear to see me die and lose You for all eternity, so You came, and on the Cross bore all my sins, my guilt, my brokenness, and my shame. Yet, I did not know it until that day when You knocked upon my door, a beggar asking only for one thing: that You may enter. You wanted to give me life. Would I accept it?

You did not chide me. You were not angry, but in Your love understood where I came from. You entered in the person of Your Son Jesus, meek and mild, teaching me like a little child until in one mighty roar the Lion of Judah appeared—no longer the gentle Jesus but the conqueror—a claimer to His throne. You fought for me on the Cross, a mighty warrior and tore down the enemy's strongholds and in one cry made this temple clean. *"My Father's house is a house of prayer an⸱ not a ⸱en of thieves!"*

In agony, I moaned as this mighty warrior thundered and roared, a jealous lover for His beloved. Valiantly You fought as the seven words tumbled from Your mouth on the Cross.

You only ask that I co-operate in Your fight. You were always on my side; I had to take mine. At each lash of the whip I was cleansed. At each moan I was freed until the new me arose in one bellowing cry, a cry for Paradise lost: *"Eli, Eli, lema Sabachthani."* Your cry on the Cross reached and touched my shattered being. The final stronghold collapsed and I was freed. Your heart full of love pierced. Yet into that wounded heart You bid me enter and drink, drink freely from the living fountain, drink freely from the Spirit.

As You were carried into the tomb You asked me to come with You. Your work was not yet over. There was a silence so deep, a death so real. I was lost, blind, and searching. Nothing could be so cold or so empty, yet the breath, the Ruah of the Father was there, His mighty Spirit remolding, forming, shaping.

Into the tomb the Spirit came, the tomb of nothingness, and the potter's hand began to form the new creation—the tomb, four stifling walls, a prison of death. Never to live or breathe again, to know the beat of the Father's heart again. Paradise lost, life lost. *"Do not be afraid, I have not abandoned you,"* You whispered to me. Your words pour out from what seems to be a lifeless corpse. Lord, You lie there motionless, covered, a cloth upon Your face. You repeat those words to me:

"*Do not be afraid.*" This waiting is like an eternity. This tomb so dark. You lie there, and yet, Your presence gives me peace. You have touched Adam within me. How he weeps for his pride. I kneel before You and even if this darkness should persist, I will remain here within this tomb with You. I touch Your wounds, Your gentle face. This is my God who died for me that I might be free, even in this tomb. You see, I never left my Father's heart; in Jesus I always lived there.

On Your Cross You became that slave for me that I might live with You for all eternity. The Great Exchange done, sins redeemed, I now know that my life is not my own. In humble submission, I whisper my 'fiat.' A mighty roar, the Father's Ruah shudders the walls of the tomb with a light so blinding. You stand there in magnificent majesty, yet so humble lest I should fear to approach. 'I AM. It is I. Do not be afraid.' Triumphantly, You lead me out of the tomb.

It is a new day, a new beginning. With Adam, I am restored. Paradise lost is now found. You bid me go tell my brothers and sisters that You are risen to heal, deliver, proclaim, restore, and bless in Your name. For, yes, You are with us until the end of time.

chapter seven
forgiveness

What is forgiveness?

To forgive is one of the hardest things we have to do. It does not come naturally, that is, to the natural man, but it is a virtue which has to be worked upon. To forgive is not weakness but strength. It is not telling someone you are free to continue to hurt me, but it is choosing to forgive, to reach out despite the hurt. It does not condone nor does it condemn; it sets you free. That is fortitude and strength. That is love. To forgive someone who hurt you is never easy, but with God it is possible. Mahatma Ghandi said that forgiveness is a virtue of the brave. Jesus forgave those who crucified Him. He forgives us every time we come to Him in the Sacrament of Reconciliation or alone. *"Father forgive them, they ⸱o not know what they are doing!*" (Luke 23:34). Forgiveness is being freed from a hurt that has been inflicted upon you. Forgiveness is facing the pain directly, acknowledging that you have been hurt, that you may feel resentment and not wanting to forgive, but you know you need to forgive. It is a decision that one makes despite our deep wounded emotions.

Why is it so important to forgive?

We forgive that we may be free.

There is a saying: "*To err is human but to forgive is divine.*"All people commit sins and make mistakes. God forgives them, and people are acting in a godlike (divine) way when they forgive.

Usually, we tend to think of forgiveness as benefiting only the one who is guilty of the wrongdoing. Viewed in this way, forgiveness is a "divine" act on the part of the one who forgives; the one who is forgiven is released of any guilt or burden and can go on with their lives, free from guilt. This is what happens in the Sacrament of Reconciliation when the Lord forgives us. This is what happens when we turn to Him and in our prayer ask for forgiveness. He wants the restoration of our relationship with Him.

But as human beings, when a person forgives another of wrong doing, does he or she benefit at all?

When it comes to forgiveness, many of us would rather hold on to our hurts, like some sort of medallion or pendant around our necks. We feel we have a right to hang onto our resentments and our angers rather than forgive the one who has done us wrong. We give reasons why we have a right to be hurt: the wrong done is too big, etc. Many reasons are strong, for the wrong doing would be deep, but we forgive in and through the Cross of Jesus Christ. It is in the power of the Holy Spirit that we are able to forgive those who have wounded us terribly.

To forgive does not mean that no wrong was done; it is not being in denial. We acknowledge the wrong done but choose to be the bigger person and forgive. It usually takes a "bigger" person to forgive. It is someone who realises that holding on to all those negative emotions only hurt them in the long run and not the person who committed the wrongdoing! We can take as an example the famous story and film of *Ben Hur*. When Ben Hur held on to his anger and unforgiveness he was turning into the very person he hated, Messala. It was only when he was face to face with Christ on the Cross and the anger and sword taken away from his hands and heart that he was able to be free and to love again. To hold on to those negative emotions creates a darkness around us which we project onto others.

When the wound is caused by someone with whom we are bound in a relationship, be it a parent, sibling, friend, relation, etc, the pain is deeper and invariably the harder to forgive. Even if it is someone not close to us at all or even unknown, we need to forgive. When we are in a relationship, hard though it may often be, for the sake of reconciliation, it must be done. There are times when a wrong done does require a break in a relationship. This does not absolve us from forgiving. Not at all. It would, however, be deemed healthier or more beneficial for the relationship to be discontinued.

To forgive is to make a decision to overcome the hurt inflicted upon us by the other person and to decide not to hold a grudge or resentment against that person. Forgiveness must always begin with a decision; the emotions come later through healing.

A life that is consumed by bitterness and resentment is a life that is being eaten away slowly from the inside. When anger and resentment consume you, this only leads to depression and a life of misery where the person can feel victimised and powerless. There would be in deep cases the element of vindictiveness and downright nastiness. Then, to feel good they would oppress and subtly or not so subtly degrade and look down on others. They begin to live out of a false life or self, live out of an ego or mask that has been created to cover their own pain.

Forgiveness gives freedom, freedom to live without the burden of the anger, resentment, and bitterness. To forgive others or ourselves for the wrong that has been committed or we have suffered because of another's or our own actions affects us emotionally, psychologically, and physically. Forgiving ourselves and others sets us free to see our own self-worth and be able to move beyond the negative feelings that are like quicksand controlling our thinking patterns and behaviour. We are free from the building up of anger and even hatred that can end up like poison within. Many people suffer from various illnesses, arthritis, chronic asthma, nervous reactive movements, depression, and or insomnia whose source is often found in resentment and unforgiveness. However, it does not necessarily mean that unforgiveness can result in these ailments. We may also have the inability to form good and healthy relationships simply because we refuse to forgive. The longer we hold onto unforgiveness the heavier the burden becomes on our hearts, minds, and souls. Instead of dwelling on all that is good and honourable and seeing the good in others, we see and feel only what is negative and dark. We are unable to live in the light.

People who do not forgive often project and transfer their hurts and angers onto others, making other people's lives unbearable. In so doing, they make them the aim of their frustrations, bitterness, and resentments. Forgiveness does not mean you have to accept the behavior of another. What is wrong is wrong. But it does mean accepting yourself, to be happy, and to move on. Forgiveness is really a gift that you give to yourself. It has very little to do with the person who has hurt you. Holding on to that hurt is like drinking poison. To forgive moves you out of that *'poor me, I am a victim'* attitude and restores your self will and ability to move forward. Forgiving others may seem to be a choice we can make or refuse to make. But if we truly want to be free, we need to understand the reality and reliability of God's Word. God has been very clear about forgiveness. He has given us specific direction in several Scripture texts, all of which can be summed up in just one word—forgive! God's Word says, "*And when you stand praying, if you hold anything against anyone, forgive him, so that your Father in heaven may forgive you your sins*" (Mark 11:25). Every time we pray the 'Our Father' we say "*… and forgive us our trespasses as we forgive those who trespass* *against us…"* We are asking the Father to forgive us, then what right do we have to withhold forgiveness to others?

Forgiveness is not a one-time happening. It is not a feeling, but a decision. The feelings can and do come over time. We make the decision to forgive, for that is what the Lord expects of us. Colossians 3:13 says, *"Bear with each other an♦ forgive whatever grievances you may have against one another. Forgive as the Lor♦ forgave you."* Sometimes even when helping others through a certain type of trauma we need to gauge when is the best time to address forgiveness. Forgiveness is ongoing. Every time we feel the hurt of the pain inflicted, we need to face it and make a conscious decision to forgive, again and again, if necessary, even though we feel like punching a hole in the wall.

When we make the decision to forgive those who have hurt us, we are removing the power from their hands to inflict more pain. We become our own persons. We take away their power. The Lord Jesus told us *"Do not ju♦ge, an♦ you will not be ju♦ge♦. Do not con♦emn, an♦ you will not be con♦emne♦. Forgive, an♦ you will be forgiven"* (Luke 6:37).

There are four areas of forgiveness that we need to know and understand.

1. To forgive others
2. To forgive ourselves

3. To forgive God

4. Receiving forgiveness

1. To forgive others

First, we need to acknowledge the pain within. Many times, we may be in denial because the knowledge of the hurt may be too much to bear. These will have to surface and be faced. We cannot work through the pain until we admit that the hurt is there and has been done. The denial may be very deep depending on the relationship. Again, we need to speak about projection or transference because if we meet people who may in some way touch a raw nerve or do something that may seem or we perceive to wound us in the way the person who initially hurt us, we lash out at them for no reason at all. We need to get to the bottom of the issue which is the lack of forgiveness and healing of the pain in the original wound. What is important to remember is that our forgiveness of the person releases that person from any strings or unhealthy ties that person may have on us. To forgive does not justify their actions, but we set them free; we set ourselves free. Our forgiveness does not take the place of God's forgiveness for their actions because only God can do that. That person has to deal with their sin with God.

The Lord helps us in this way to come in touch with our pain and to release forgiveness. We would need to enter into the healing of memories and allow the Holy Spirit to touch and heal the initial wound or source of the trauma. We need to face the persons in our prayer when we are in the presence of the Lord and slowly let the Lord lead us to release forgiveness even when it is hard. The Lord wants to free us to live as children of the Father.

2. To forgive ourselves

Maybe one of the most hidden problems we need to face is the need to forgive ourselves. A lot of the times when we have done something wrong, we may have confessed our sin but the lingering guilt or shame remains. In certain delicate situations, we may be experiencing a false guilt when the fault is not ours but placed upon us. This is especially felt when there has been any form of abuse be it sexual, emotional, psychological, or physical. In other cases, the wound can be so deep that we are unable to touch it alone. We may need someone to walk with us, to pray with us, to be with us in our need and pain. We need the help of the Holy Spirit to gently lead us to the wound, and it is with His love that we can face our own pain. The Lord did not come to condemn but to save us (John 3:17). We need to forgive ourselves for, indeed, the Lord has already forgiven us.

To forgive oneself is a very hard process and requires a lot of love and acceptance especially of the spiritual companion or counsellor. The pain of self-rejection, self-hatred may even surface. I have often used the mirror as a help in this. Asking the person to face themselves in the mirror especially when they are raw, more often than not they cannot at this point in time. Then when they actually do and are able to face themselves in the mirror, we pray for the Holy Spirit to come and to help release forgiveness to themselves as though to another person. The Lord works deeply and though the pain is very deep, it takes a lot of love and time to release and cleanse this deep wound. We pray for the power and Blood of Christ to cleanse the wound completely of anything, especially if there is a spirit of unforgiveness present and to set free His child.

There may also be the need to forgive the inner child. Again, we need to place the child at that particular age in front of us and release forgiveness. We shall deal with this later on.

3. To forgive God

Now you may say no one needs to forgive God, for the Lord has done nothing wrong. This is all very true in every sense of the word. The Lord saved us and did not come to hurt us. He has taken all our pain and suffering, all our sin and our inability to forgive upon His Cross. But unfortunately, part of our wrong teaching has been that the Lord sends us crosses and disasters and we have become accustomed to blaming the Lord from anything to everything. We even have our insurance covers that do not cover 'acts of God.' If there is a war, we blame Him. If there is a famine, we blame Him. If a child dies, we blame Him. We pray and if things do not go our way, we blame Him. Why? The truth is, we do not really need to forgive God but to let go of our accusation towards Him.

So, let us try to understand why we transfer and project our broken hearts and blame onto the Lord.

We know that the Lord is love and that He is good. He loves us, cares for us, and provides for us. He is the Almighty and the Omnipotent, but He is also Father. However, when we are in pain, when we are faced with a tragic situation in our family, we turn to Him to help us out. When things do not go the way we expect them to go, we blame Him saying He does not care; He does not hear us. A lot of times we accuse Him of not being there when we needed Him. Why did He not stop that car accident? Why did He not stop that abuser when He could? So, our angers are flared up towards Him. We hold Him up in court and in accusation once again. The truth is, sin is to be blamed for we do not know the Lord's ways. We are not in tune or in right relationship with Him to be able to surrender in a true way. Let us admit, we are all on a journey towards His heart. So, when we are in this state, we need to acknowledge that we need not so much as to forgive God but to let go of our accusation towards Him.

First, we need to acknowledge our pain, anxieties, and fears. We need to acknowledge that we hold the Lord in accusation and why? What are we accusing Him of? Then we need to allow the Holy Spirit to help us go to the Cross and place our accusation there. In addressing our accusation towards the Lord, we realise that He is the one helping us to go forward, and it is then that forgiveness comes. He comes to heal the wound. Many people blame Him for the injustices in their lives, for their problems and hurts. Imagine a little child who is hurting. The father has done something which the child cannot understand and holds the father responsible for his or her suffering. The child is angry towards the father, yet the father, though hurting, seeing the child's pain in their outbursts and even rebellion and disobedience, knows that all of this is borne out of the suffering. He knows and understands the pain of the child. When the child comes face to face with his or her anger and pain, the child will hurl out at the father and then break down only to realise that the father is comforting him or her and helping him or her to move forward. It is then that the child sees the truth of his or her misplaced accusation and unforgiveness and turns to the father seeking comfort, tenderness, and forgiveness.

4. Receiving forgiveness

We have spoken a lot about releasing forgiveness but not about receiving forgiveness. One of the obstacles of not being able to receive forgiveness is, we think or feel that our sin is too big and cannot be forgiven. We may be scrupulous; we doubt the love of God and/or we cannot forgive ourselves. Or else we are deep in pride in a way that does not allow the Lord's forgiveness and His compassion to touch us. There could also be a negative bondage, but this would require discernment and prayer. We may even think we do not need to receive the Lord's forgiveness or anyone else's for that matter. We have never learned to say *Sorry, I was wrong!*

To receive forgiveness is to place oneself in a place of being in the wrong, and allowing, in humility, another to forgive you for any wrong you may have done or perceived to have done. When we are able to receive forgiveness, we receive the freedom of Christ and the strength to move forward in life. When we receive and are able to receive forgiveness from a friend or a person in relationship, there is a strengthening of the true bond which more often than not is deeper and stronger than the relationship was previously.

Let us look at two people: One who was not able to receive forgiveness and despaired and the other who did receive forgiveness, repented, and moved on. One was Judas. He despaired of his sin and felt that he could not be pardoned. Jesus loved him, but Judas could not receive that love. His despair shut out the possibility of receiving the love and forgiveness Jesus wanted to give him. We know what he did. He was the example of a man in despair over sin. The other was Peter. He, too, sinned but in the repentance was able to receive the Lord's forgiveness, acknowledge his weakness and with the love of the community and Jesus, could stand up and walk again. The Lord Jesus re-instated him as the leader and head of the Church (John 21).

A true picture of beautiful forgiveness is the parable of the Prodigal son. We need to receive and experience the Father's forgiveness. God the Father is not just waiting for us, but as in the parable, He runs out to meet us. *"The Lord waits to be gracious to you; he exalts himself to show mercy to you"* (Isaiah 30:18). When He sees us coming to Him, He runs out to meet us. There is no reservation in His heart towards us, for He is totally forgiving. He does not condone our rebellion or selfishness, for it grieves Him deeply to see us hurting ourselves and others. When we have done wrong, we know it, and we need to repent. It is His grief, His broken heart, His compassion, and His willingness to give us so much love that finally breaks through the doors of our stubborn and hardened hearts. To know the Lord is to love Him, and to love Him is to obey Him.

When all is said and done, we need to look to the Lord and do what He tells us. *"But I say to you, Love your enemies, bless those that curse you, ·o goo· to those that hate you, an· pray for those who speak evil about you, an· persecute you"* (Mark 5:44).

We have seen the importance of forgiveness and the dangers of unforgiveness. Nothing is impossible for the Lord. There is no pain or wound that cannot be touched and healed by the Holy Spirit.

chapter eight

the Lord strengthens and renews my inner being

Ephesians 3:16-20: *"I pray that according to the riches of his glory he may grant you to be strengthened with might through his Spirit in the inner man (your inner person), and that Christ may dwell in your hearts through faith; that you, being rooted and grounded in love, may have power to comprehend with all the saints what is the breadth and length and height and depth, and to know the love of Christ which surpasses knowledge, that you may be filled with all the fullness of God. Now to him who by the power at work within us is able to do far more abundantly than all that we ask or think, to him be glory in the church an♦ in Christ Jesus to all generations, for ever an♦ ever. Amen."*

The Lord heals us through the power of the Cross. We enter into the Cross and in this love, we allow Him to take us into the tomb of Saturday and out into the light of the Resurrection. All that is incarnate within us, that is, our created being, our emotional, psychological, spiritual, and physical being needs healing. We are persons who wounded by original sin and by the effects of sin need to be healed. Unfortunately, we have not realised to what extent we need healing. We are faced with a lot of obvious situations whether in our marriages, families, relationships, place of work, but we never or may not journey deep into the depths to discover the roots of our problems to bring to the Cross of Christ and allow Him to heal the wounds.

Now I ask you, what of your journey inwards? Do we consider our inward journey? If we are not on the journey then we are moving backwards. To move forward is to journey in Christ and it is to choose life. It is to choose truth, not only doctrinal truth, not only spiritual truth, but truth within ourselves. It is to leave the old self behind and be healed through the Cross of Christ in the power of His Spirit. It is to discover what is and what is not of God deep within and to ask the Spirit to enable us to change, to effect change within, and to take the necessary decisions and actions needed. *Metanoia* (repentance) a turning around, a change of direction, of heart is required.

If we do not make this journey, we will be like a bunch of dead bones, people who think that they are alive in Christ but are not. We must move forward so that streams of living waters and the truth of Christ, the Spirit, that is forever fresh, brings us new life and insight into our deep being.

We need to be more aware of what is happening within us for we are called to live on the deeper level. As persons we are complicated beings, but we are human beings made in the image and likeness of God, created by God for His glory and our salvation. There is within our deepest being a great desire for oneness, for wholeness, for God is the WHOLE ONE; HE IS THE HOLY ONE.

We can speak of the different dimensions of human existence which is the outer circle that is external behaviour, then the secondary level which relates to the emotional and reasoning level, and the core level which is where the true person, that is, where the true me lives. We could, in spiritual terms, refer this to the level of our external and natural humanity, then the soul level and our deep spirit, the human spirit where the Holy Spirit dwells. It is in this core, in this deep spirit level that Christ has taken His abode in me. This is where He dwells within me. From this deep inner core Christ reaches out and heals and restores all the other levels within. He makes me whole and tells me who I truly am. This is where the real me, all that I am in Christ lives. It is here, it is this ME that Christ wants to release and set free to become all that I am called to be.

We are called to be conscious of who we are on a psychological as well as a spiritual level, on the psychological or reasoning level so that we can understand ourselves better and work towards our goal. Then on the spiritual level, we are to be in touch with ourselves which is at the deepest level of our being.

So, let us go on this journey to the centre, not of the earth, but to the centre of me. I am reminded of a beautiful song sung by Charlene in 1982 *'I have never been to me.'* Have you been to you? Do you know the real you? Are you living out of the real you or are you living on a superficial level that is not the real you? Are you in bondage to the world, to its demands, to others? Or are you a child, a free child of Christ, a servant of the Word? Have you discovered the true and real you? This is discernment on a different level, a different perspective. The truth of Christ is shining deep within so that I can see who I am and allow the Spirit to effect change within me. He will help you change and strengthen you in your inner being.

The Holy Spirit leads us on this, our journey forward, our journey to ME, to who I am in Christ so that we might know and be rooted and grounded in the love of Christ as St. Paul tells us in his letter to the Ephesians.

The natural human level

Let us start our journey on this natural human level, the superficial level of the person where the behaviours, features, anything that is external is visible.

This is the immediate image we have of a person. The way the person smiles, laughs, holds their body, whether the person speaks fast or slow—now let us be honest, do we often judge people on these criteria?

Then taking this a bit further, do we live on this level? If you had to go into an office, shop, or church and you see someone you do not know very well, what is your first thought? You look at the person. You immediately think of what that person is and you have labeled that person. What the person is wearing, how he or she is sitting, tattoos or not, jewellery, make-up—we have immediately sized up the person. If the person looks okay to us, we shall say 'good morning.' If we feel that we do not like the person we won't even look at them. What if a person had to come to you dressed in rags or tatty clothes, how would you treat that person? Would you treat that person with the same dignity as someone who is well dressed? That shows up what we are and this is what the Lord wants to change in us. This shows the attitudes of our hearts. We may not speak it, but we live it, and it is these things that the Lord wants to change.

This is a very superficial level. We want to conform to the world and we end up pleasing the world. Now we know that the world, meaning the love of the things and attitudes of the world are at enmity with God. We are living out of the old man—the natural self—and this needs to change and be healed.

So, are we living our lives on this level? We want to flow with the crowd or our surroundings without discerning the roads we are taking. This is trying to be *'people pleasers instead of a God pleaser?'* Is my image, my appearance, meaning my ego, so important that it suffocates the truth not only of God and the Gospel but the truth within me?

Are we so afraid or ruled by what people say about us that we bend ourselves backwards to be liked, to be approved of, that we conform to the world around us, to society around us? What of truth? To be with Christ often means going against, swimming against the current. No one said it was easy, but we need to recognise it so that we can start walking in the way of truth.

There is a lot to think about. The light of Christ now shines on this area of our lives. This is the topmost soil, so to say. It is the outer circle of our being.

The second or inner level

Then there is the interior level or circle. This refers to our feelings, our way of thinking, our mentality, emotions, reactions, instincts, and attractions, even impulsiveness—I feel it, I do it. We do not think or discern. Here, we may be easily offended. Our thought patterns change according to our feelings. What we need is to put on the mind and heart of Christ. This fluctuating inner level is not necessarily the real and true me, but it is my deep reaction to my surroundings, to the world outside. These are my responses, my moods and instincts. It is what we do with these reactions that become our moral ground. Here our levels of interaction take on a different moral criteria. Many times, we confuse the intensity of these feelings and think that it is something spiritual. They would be our emotions on a deep level. That is why discernment is so important, for to be impulsive and dependent on one's feelings alone can lead to radical mistakes.

Do we live out of what we feel, out of our instincts especially on the moral level? What we do can then become and turn into sin. Or do we have self-control, a fruit of the Holy Spirit? Do we have forbearance and patience? We need to wait upon the Lord and listen to Him. The way we think, our thought patterns come from the heart and form us. Nobody can see the thought patterns of the mind. If people could read your mind, when they see you they may say, *'Oh, I know what you are thinking.'* We can have an idea even through body language, but no one can read the mind for only you know your thought patterns. Paul tells us *"put on the mine of Christ"* (Philippians 2:5-8). We have to think as Christ thinks. There must be a complete rewiring of the mind. We need healing in our attitudes, in our emotions, and in our thought patterns.

There is the saying *'What I do and say, I become.'*

This is true of habits. Do we cultivate good habits so that they become virtues or are our habits becoming vices? I can be angry, but do I react in anger to a point where it becomes sin? This is the moral level of our being and a lot of our lives are lived on this level. What of the fruits of the Spirit? Are they being formed within us?

This level is also formed through our upbringing, schooling, ways and attitudes of reasoning, the values we hold onto, and to what we give value and importance to. These need healing and restoration in the Holy Spirit.

As we allow the Gospel and the Word of God to shine its light at a deep level, it is here we have the level of change. The Cross of Christ brings salvation, and it is on this level that we can change a lot in our life and deal with what is negative. It is this level that affects the outer level. The deeper we dive and allow the light and Blood of the Cross to touch this inner level of our being, the more we are healed and transformed. It is here that we can see and discern as to what enslaves us and how we are formed.

Are we responsible persons? Are we responsible morally? To be responsible morally does not mean only sexually, but also in business, in money, in our attitudes towards others, in my responsibilities, in my work, in my marital relationship, and in my relationship with my children, friends, and colleagues, and even in the way I look after myself.

When we say looking after ourselves or loving ourselves, we are not meaning egocentricity, but to have a healthy Gospel attitude even towards oneself; that is also a great moral issue. God the Father loves all He has created and that includes me!

Sometimes we think, Yes, He loves everyone but me. This is a fallacy and a lie of the evil one. We are precious and unique to Him. Self-pity, bringing oneself down is not Gospel humility but rather a strong egoism at work. The same is said for the egocentric lifestyle, the hedonist, the person who is so self-indulgent and selfish. But how can we love ourselves, we ask? Unless we know that the Lord loves us, how can we love our neighbours as Christ wants us to, if we do not love ourselves? The Lord's love for us is unconditional, for *"his love has been poure* into our hearts through the Holy Spirit"* (Romans 5:5). He asks of us that we *"*o unto others as you woul* have *one unto you"* (Luke 6:31; Matthew 7:12). How would you like people to treat you? You would like them to welcome you, to feed you if you are hungry, to speak to you if you are alone, to forgive you and have compassion upon you.

When we look to Him and are silent in listening prayer with the Lord, the Holy Spirit reveals Himself and myself to me. What is influencing me? Is it the Gospel of Christ or the pulls of the world? What is guiding me? What has deeply wounded my life? Why do I continuously move or talk in a negative way? What are the patterns that are formed within? We need to be aware, yes, very much aware at this level for this is a very important and life-changing level. Self-awareness is necessary for us to grow. These are the attitudes of the heart. We may not speak them, but they are there for they show themselves in the way we act and react.

The Gospel of Christ speaks to us and does transform us, if we allow it to. We are called to be made new, to be transformed in Christ through the power of the Cross, if we allow the Word to speak deeply into our hearts and the Holy Spirit to truly change us. As I change on this level, I can then enter more deeply and be more in touch with my inner core, my spirit level where I and Christ truly dwell.

This level is very important for my spiritual and psychological life and maturity.

On this level we should not be living off our natural emotions; that is the first level. Our emotions are good, God-given, and must be healed. We should be in control of our lives, our emotions, our feelings, and the way we speak and relate to others. To be spontaneous does not mean I can shoot my mouth off, but rather I can rejoice and be free in who I am in Christ. We live by the fruits of the Spirit and this includes self-control. To be in the Spirit does not mean that we do whatever comes to mind or what we feel. Discernment is necessary. Some people think that they are being sincere when they speak whatever comes into their heads or hearts; they have no reign over their tongues! In James 3:5-9, we see that the tongue is a very small but powerful organ. How many of us have been wounded by the tongue of another? I can safely say we all have. We use the tongue to praise God, yet we use our tongue to hurt others. We use our tongue to blaspheme and to curse. The tongue, as the Letter of James chapter three tells us, is a small organ which can set alight a forest fire. Jesus tells us, the mouth speaks of what is in the heart. So, when an abuse, gossip, or slander comes out of the tongue that thought was already in the heart and here is where we link the attitudes, the heart, and the tongue together.

This kind of attitude, this lack of emotional discipline makes us slaves of our emotions and feelings. Do we react when someone says something we do not like? Do we lash back? Are we quick-tongued, or do we think and reason out in faith praying before we say anything that might cause immense damage? We need to have meekness of the Spirit which is a disciplined and discerning spirit. Meekness is representative of a well-balanced emotional person.

Do we have the wisdom and understanding when to speak or not to speak? Here on this level we develop our character and personality that we might live as free persons and children of the Father. This is what true freedom in Christ is.

The inner core/the Spirit

Now we come to the inner core, or the place where the Spirit dwells, which is the centre. We have travelled down the different levels of our being and now enter into the very centre, the core of who we are.

Who Am I? Who Am I in Christ?

This inner core is the Spiritual level.

Many of us do not even touch this area, let alone live out of it.

It is here that Jesus Christ, the Spirit of God dwells, and it is in this place that I Am, that I truly Am who I Am. Created in God's image and likeness it is here that this image lives. When God in Genesis said that everything is good, all that He created is good, when He said that man and woman are good, it is here that He means that all is good, in this place and abode.

It is here that the very decisive and serious moral choices are made. We can either grieve the Spirit of God or block Him, or we can grow more in Him. We who profess Christ have a great awareness of what we are doing and hence a greater responsibility before God for our actions.

It is here that we can and are free, and it is from this place that we are capable of true love, sacrificial love, and self-giving. Here Gospel love finds its place. The Gospel is and should be in its right place here. St. Augustine said *"Our heart is restless until it finds its rest in You."* It is here that the soul is at rest and finds its peace and fullness in Christ. We may have turmoil on the other levels, but peace and joy at core level in our spirit. Here are the deep waters of the Spirit.

This is the place of Agape love, the place where the fruits abound and where holiness springs forth. This is where the streams of living water flow out of us and onto those around us. In this place where the inner streams of living water flow, lie the treasures like gem stones hidden in the rock surface. Only the eyes accustomed to this inner place can feel the coolness of the water and discern the glint of the gems embedded in the rock. As we grow, we begin to discern and are able to live from this deep inner place no matter what is happening on the other levels. We are like stars shooting up and out into life with the freshness of the Spirit.

As we grow in Christ, we are to be aware of what is happening on all these three levels. We see the change and movements within us. We are to discern what is going on and how the Spirit is moving within our being, both on the psychological and spiritual levels. On these levels we discern where and what is giving us resistance, what we find so hard, and where evil may be lurking within. The eyes of the soul are alive and can see what the ordinary eyes cannot see. This is the place where we can either shut the doors to the Spirit of God or where we find that we can flow more easily.

We must discern where we see the EGO, that is, the big 'I' that is forever wanting to rear its head. We must learn to die to self and learn to overcome difficulties in Christ. We will also see and discern the movements of what is good and bad or even evil within us. We take our decisions, take action and move towards the good that is Christ.

What is most important is that we do not despair or lose hope for Christ is our hope, and it is in His love that we overcome all obstacles to our growth of holiness in Him. Ephesians 3:16-20:

So *being rooted and grounded in love, we may have **power to comprehend** (to discern and understand) with all the saints, (that is us) what is the breadth and length and height and depth, and **to know** (to experience) the love of Christ (which is deep within us) which surpasses knowledge, that we may be **filled with all the fullness of God** (that is on all three levels). Now to him who **by the power at work within us** (the Spirit who is at the core of our being) is able to do far more abundantly **than all that we ask or think** (the Lord wants our healing and holiness much more than we do), to him be glory in **the church** (for we are all brothers and sisters in Christ and how we act and relate affects others and those around me) and* *in Christ Jesus **to all generations** (how I am and act affects my children and grandchildren etc), for ever and ever. Amen.*

chapter nine
Christ comes to heal our traumas and our memories

The Lord alone is our strength. He is our salvation. It is in Him that we find rest for our souls, our hearts, and our minds. It is in His love that all our pain and sorrows are healed and we find our restoration.

"Blessed are they that mourn, for they shall be comforted." (Matthew 5:4).

Psalm 139:1-6: *"O LORD, you search me and you know me! You know when I sit down and when I rise up; you discern my thoughts from afar. You search out my path and my lying down, and are acquainted with all my ways. Even before a word is on my tongue, lo, O LORD, you know it altogether. You hem me in from* behin• an• before, an• lay your han• upon me. Such knowle•ge is too won•erful for me; it is high, I cannot attain it."

A lot of the roots of our pain and suffering do not lie on the surface but are buried deep within our subconscious having their toll and affect in our present everyday life, in the way we speak, act, respond, relate, etc. This takes the form of repressed memories which though suppressed are linked to a particular trauma we would have experienced in our lives. When we mention trauma, one might immediately think of something very tragic or disastrous; however, this is not the case. It is not only those very tragic happenings that can affect our lives, but even particular small singular events or ongoing circumstances can have a massive impact on our deep conscious and, hence, affect us even today.

It is in those moments of pain that Jesus Christ is present. Jesus is the I AM. There is no time in Christ. He is present at that moment as much as He is present now and will be present to all of us until the end of time. The Lord is outside the human time frame which is *kronos* time.

What causes emotional and psychological trauma?

Emotional and psychological trauma is the result of extraordinarily stressful events that shatter our sense of security, making us feel helpless and vulnerable in the world around us. Trauma can also stem from ongoing, relentless stress, ongoing sickness in oneself or the family, any situation that affects us at the core of our being. These situations are then stored in the depth of the sensory part of our brains, the emotional brain. Biblically speaking, we would refer to this as the depth of our being, the heart, which covers the emotional, psychological, and thinking process of the human person.

Tragic traumatic experiences often involve some threatening situation in our life or a threat to our safety. In fact, any situation that leaves us feeling overwhelmed and alone can be traumatic, even if it does not involve physical harm. It is not the objective facts that determine whether an event is traumatic, but how the experience of the event affects us emotionally and psychologically. The more frightened and helpless we feel, the more likely we are to be traumatized. That is why children who are so vulnerable can be traumatised so easily.Below are some of the events that can cause emotional or psychological trauma:

- It happened unexpectedly.
- A person we have trusted suddenly abuses that trust deeply.
- We felt powerless to prevent it.
- It happened repeatedly.
- Someone was intentionally cruel.
- It happened in childhood.

Though not all potentially traumatic situations can lead to emotional or psychological trauma, each person is affected differently. We can be quite affected even though on the surface this may not seem to be the case.

Childhood trauma can and does, in most cases, have a long-term effect. When these have not been resolved, the effects overflow into our adult life creating a bed for further trauma.

Below are some childhood experiences that may cause trauma and unsettle the child's sense of safety and security:

- An unstable or unsafe environment
- Separation from a parent
- Separation or divorce of the parents
- Sudden death in the family
- Serious illness
- Intrusive medical procedures
- Accidents
- Sexual, physical, or verbal abuse
- Domestic violence
- Neglect
- Bullying

When a trauma affects us we can feel a myriad of things:

- Shock, denial, or disbelief
- Anger, irritability, mood swings
- Guilt, shame, self-blame
- Feeling sad or hopeless
- Confusion, difficulty concentrating
- Anxiety and fear
- Withdrawing from others
- Feeling disconnected or numb

We can also be affected physically affected:

- Insomnia or nightmares
- Being startled easily
- Racing heartbeat
- Aches and pains
- Migraines
- Wanting to sleep all the time
- Fatigue
- Eating disorders
- Difficulty concentrating
- Edginess and agitation
- Muscle tension
- High blood pressure

As human beings we react to these situations. However, we realise that our emotional and psychological being needs healing. We may have to seek professional medical help. Nonetheless, even in these cases, we need the help of the Lord Jesus to come and walk with us, to heal us. To heal from psychological and emotional trauma, we must face and resolve the unbearable feelings, memories, and unresolved pain we have long avoided; otherwise, they will return again and again, unbidden and uncontrollable.

We have within us a deeply embedded belief system forming our understanding of who and what we are and what we see around us. We are sensitised to our surroundings, circumstances, events, and to the details of our lives. At the centre of the memory of a trauma is a deeply entrenched negative belief or thought pattern. That belief or thought pattern becomes embedded within our emotional and psychological being when we experience an intense situation. For it is in intense states and situations like fear, horror, pain, anxiety, etc. that we are open and made vulnerable to receive, like a dagger, those words, scenes, and actions that affect and traumatise us. What we are told and what we believe become embedded and form a web of beliefs that will not allow reason or basic understanding to release it. We become captives to those beliefs and begin to truly live out of them. We then believe and become what we are not. We believe that all these negative symptoms and feelings are the true me, that this is who I am.

But this is not who I am; this is not the real me. This is the dragon of the trauma inside of me not letting the real me live, taking over my life in such a way that I cannot be free. It will not let me find my true identity. I am meant to be free and live and be all that Christ wants me and plans for me to be.

These moments are embedded in our emotions in such a way that when we are under stress, they surface like a deep-sea water monster, large as life, greatly influencing us. These memories alongside the negative feelings lead our beliefs, perceptions, and understanding especially when certain wounds have been touched, when we are vulnerable, or when we are under stress. The trouble is they are so embedded that they take over our thoughts and actions. We need healing as we just cannot wish them or reason them away. Time does not heal these wounds, even though we may have forgotten about them, for they will surface one day when a situation, word, or action triggers the memory or squeezes and releases the unhealed emotions. If the memory is nearer our consciousness, that is, we do have a living memory of it, we may just learn how to live in this situation. However, this is not the ideal, for our lives will, whether we like it or not, be hinged and linked to that situation, word, memory, etc.

The reality is, it becomes like poison to our inner being and when these wounds are touched, we react even in the most ordinary situations. Our life image becomes distorted and our vision and perception clouded. Our world view is seen through the suppressed memory of the trauma, and we act out of these beliefs, believing them to be who we truly are or else seeing into situations things that are not. When under stress, anxiety, or a deep emotional upheaval, whatever we perceive, whatever we are told or we tell ourselves becomes a reality and truth even though they may be lies and deceit. We misconceive the best intentions and we then believe and live out of this lie. This trauma then affects our life in its many aspects. We begin to project and transfer those negative emotions onto others whenever we see something similar that initially caused our pain or hurt. What we believe in our heart is then often spoken out loud reaffirming our deep woundedness, for our belief system has now been diseased, and sadly very often what was done to us and how we perceive ourselves, we do and are to others.

When we become anxious, ultra-stressed, and fearful we can be open to panic attacks. These can be accompanied by feelings of worthlessness, hopelessness, depression, discouragement. There could also be burdens of false guilt or the feeling of everything being our fault when it is not. All of these feelings will have their roots in the trauma. On the flip side, we could react and lash out onto others becoming malicious, ultra-critical, or abusive. The root cause lies in the depth of our being.

But the Lord comes; He comes to save and to heal us.

As we have initially mentioned, we have what is termed an emotional brain which stores all these elements within it. What the trauma does is affect this emotional brain and feed it with all these negative feelings and beliefs. This emotional brain remembers and stores all the emotional and psychological events in our lives both the good and the negative. These beliefs affect our lives and more importantly what we believe and understand about our identity and the character of God and those relationships we hold dear. These, many times, need to be forgiven and set free. The Lord comes to set us free from the broken self, the areas of the broken self that we might live in the truth of life in Him. It is through the healing of these traumas that the Lord comes and makes us new in Him.

These traumas and their effects do not go away with time; they need to be identified, brought to the Lord, and healed for Christ wants us to build our lives on His Word that is a rock under our feet. This is the truth that sets us free.

Healing our memories

To be healed from emotional and psychological trauma we need to heal the memories. This would mean touching and opening the wound to heal the trauma-related memories and feelings. This is a process. In this process, we will come in touch with a *"fight or flight"* dynamism that releases very strong emotions. Within this is the sense of the loss of trust which needs to be rebuilt.

We also feel within us a sense of loss, of having lost something very dear. The natural reaction to this loss is grief. To come out of trauma involves an element of grief. There is a grieving process until we begin to stabilise and are healed.

When we have come to the place of the healing of memories, we need to come to a place of trust in the Lord for

His Word tells us *"He has sent me to bin♦ up the broken hearte♦, to proclaim free♦om for the captives an♦ release from ♦arkness for the prisoners"* (Isaiah 61:1). Very often the healing of memories starts from flashbacks. This is the surfacing of the wounded memory. They can be swift or move in very slow motion. They may even come up as symbolic images, sometimes dark and negative for the heart retains and speaks in symbols. Rest assured that if this memory has surfaced and the pain is there, it means that the Lord wants to heal it and bring us to a deeper place of healing. If it is a childhood memory, it is the child within crying out for healing. We shall deal with the healing of the inner child further on. It is important to remember that where there is trauma, very often there is the need of forgiveness which comes as one of the last stages of healing. This might also mean reaffirming the forgiveness that has already been released. This cleanses the wound that it may heal.

In the healing of memories and the effects of trauma, though the conscious mind may forget, the emotional brain, the subconscious, the heart does not. One of the first steps to healing is to come out of denial and call the event or sin by its name, whether we have sinned or have been sinned against. Our mind, that is our intellect, will try to reason things out, even to suppress or play down the damage done. This stands in contrast to the 'heart,' the core of our feeling being, the 'emotional brain.' The heart is the seat of the memory, the emotional brain, and it is the heart that thinks in symbols, images, or pictures.

Bernard Lonergan says, "*It is an image of a real or imaginary object that evokes a feeling or is evoke• by a feeling.*" At times, we will need insight and a deep understanding of what is happening. These feelings often rise up unexpectedly and with them certain images. When the images or memory is released, the flash backs and the images come to the fore. In the healing process there is no time element. It is here that the Lord comes in to heal. Though we are creatures of time, Christ is not, and He is present at that particular moment to bring healing. What is happening deep within the experience of that wound has an effect on our soul, mind, and spirit. If we are in a state of control or being prayed with, we ask the Lord to enter into that time element to bring His healing. The use of our imagination is also important for we call upon the Lord to come into that place of woundedness. He speaks to us and touches our wounds. This form of therapy, called *Christo-therapy* has brought and brings a lot of healing to those broken by trauma and in need of the healing of memories.

Christ does not only heal the memory but goes to the root to uproot the diseased parasite that has wound its tentacles of negative voices, thought patterns, and wrong self-image in our soul. Sometimes the healing may also involve the deliverance of a negative spirit that has entered through trauma and embedded itself in the diseased wound, creating havoc in the person's life. These need to be identified one by one and brought up and out onto the Cross of Christ through healing prayer. Throughout the healing prayer we need to verbalise the words, at times even vomit out the words or actions that need to be healed. Christ is there within with His axe cutting at the roots of our trauma and brokenness, making us whole.

Listening prayer

In our own prayer time, through listening prayer, we, too, can enter into the presence of the Lord and ask Him to come and to heal a memory or wound. The Father knows us. He is our creator. He knows everything about us: our complete history, present, and future. He is not bound by time. He knew us before we were even born and saw every influence upon our life. He alone totally understands our body, our emotions, our psychological functioning, our thinking, our actions, and our reactions. For the Psalmist says, "*We are fearfully an• won•erfully ma•e*" (Psalm 139:14). We are created to be healed and made whole in Christ. We are to be renewed.

If we have negative feelings but no memory, then we can ask the Lord to bring up the memory so it can be healed. Many times, we have an intense feeling, have intense reactions that are not in proportion to an event that has evoked those feelings. As we said earlier, there is the likelihood of an emotional trauma embedded in our memory. Our emotional brain has recorded the root and the actual event. Jesus comes to set us free, to set the captives free from the chains that bind us; in this case, the chains caused by a traumatic memory.

If we are unable to visualise, it is likely that we will then sense the scene, sense the presence of Jesus with us. It is at this time that we can also converse with the Lord, cry out to Him our pain, anger, and frustration and let Him deal with the situation. In so doing, we are allowing Him into those negative embedded thought patterns, beliefs, and understanding which are to be exchanged for the truth received by listening to Jesus' healing and affirming Word, to His love, and to the Word of God found in the Scriptures. Then we can visualise Jesus speaking to us and ministering to our needs. We receive peace and a deeper sense of being loved. In so doing, Jesus is '*re-wiring,*' so to say, our emotional brain, establishing a new and fresh condition wherein God's truth can be better received and the lies destroyed by the light and truth of the sword of God's

Word. As we pray in this way, we create a picture of the relevant Biblical truths, beginning with God's love and the presence of the Holy Spirit within us. We are those who have received God's forgiveness and salvation. He is the source of the truth that will lead to healing *"For the Spirit of truth will guiɛe us into all the truth"* (John 16:13).

God's living Word is the double-edged sword that is 'alive and active.' He pours His Word of Life into our brokenness and His Word heals and changes us. His Word is active and effective, and it transforms our beliefs and images in our emotional brain. The negative symbols are then changed and transformed into symbols of goodness and light. We will have wholesome and biblical symbols as given to us in our Judeo-Christian heritage.

When we pray, we pray for truth and wisdom, and listen for God's answers, following the Lord's healing direction. No one hears God perfectly, so it is important to understand that both the person being prayed with and the pray-er have their own various thoughts and pictures in combination with God's wisdom. When the ideas we hear are from God, they will never go against Biblical truth because God does not contradict Himself. Prayer is not a one-time event and needs to continue throughout the counselling process.

This visual imagery is a powerful spiritual tool to release anxiety from trauma. It gives peace about truth and creates hope and direction for the next step of healing. *"I wait patiently for the Lord; he turned to me and heard my cry. He lifted me out of the slimy pit, he set my feet upon a rock and gave me a firm place to stand. He put a new song in my mouth"* (Psalm 40:1-3). *"Those who hope in the Lord will renew their strength. They will soar on wings like eagles; they will run and not grow weary, they will walk and not be faint"* (Isaiah 40:31). People who in their pain come to know God the Father as strong, trustworthy, saving, and loving, can often shorten their healing period. The road to wholeness is unique for each person with the Lord who directs and counsels us for each step of the way.

One thing we need to be aware of is that we need to also discern these memory images since the psychological perception and other emotional factors can be involved in such a way that though the image may be correct, the proper root needs to be discerned well. Also, when possible, verification of certain events may need to be made.

chapter ten
the healing of the inner child

In each of us, there is a young, suffering child. We have all experienced difficulties of one form or another as children, and many of us have experienced trauma. To protect and defend ourselves against future suffering we may have set up high walls or formed very strong defence mechanisms. We often try to forget those painful times and will not allow ourselves to experience the suffering, believing that we cannot handle or bear it. We, therefore, suppress our feelings and memories deep down in our unconscious mind. It may be that we have not dared face this child for a long time.

But just because we may have ignored the child within, this does not mean he or she is not there. The wounded child is always there, clamouring for our attention. Often this is perceived when the adult acts in a certain way or whose speech and attitude is childish in such a way or at certain times that it is not in line with their age or role in life. Another indication is if the person is constantly seeking attention, literally like a child and reacts negatively if he or she does not get it. We want to end our suffering by sending the child to a deep place inside, creating a separation from the child and the adult. Suppressing this inner child will not heal the trauma but prolong and increase it.

The wounded child asks for our love and care, but we recoil and reject the child, doing the very opposite. The pain and sorrow in us feel overwhelming. Even if we have time, we do not come home to ourselves. We keep ourselves constantly on the go. We do not want to be still and be present to the child within us because we do not want to experience that suffering all over again. The wounded child is alive in our very being. We do not have to look far into the past for that child; we only have to look deeply and we can be in touch with him or her. The suffering of that wounded child is lying inside us at the present moment.

As we listen compassionately to others, we must also listen to the wounded child within us. We need to tenderly embrace the child, talk directly to the child within us, even asking forgiveness for having neglected her or him.

Be present to the child within you. Ask Jesus to come and sit and talk to your inner child. We know how Jesus chided the apostles for stopping the children from coming to Him. Both you and Jesus embrace and love the child, encourage and speak tenderly, asking the child what are the pains that hurt him or her so that the both of you—you and Jesus—can deal with the hurt and pain. Talking to your inner child daily brings much healing and, in many cases, heals the trauma.

It is through the healing of the inner child, the grieving of the wounds that have been suffered that our behaviour patterns can be changed and our emotional processes changed. All those pent-up emotions, that shame, anger, terror, sense of rejection, all coming from those wounds within are to be released from within. The wounds that need healing can be the result of another person's action or of certain circumstance in our lives. In the process of the healing of the inner child, grief is the main emotion that can remain throughout.For the inner child to be healed we need to heal the memories. This would mean touching and opening the wound to heal the trauma-related memories and feelings. This is a process. In this process, we will come in touch with a *"fight or flight"* dynamism that releases very strong emotions. Within this is the sense of the loss of trust which needs to be rebuilt. When we have come to the place of the healing of memories we need to come to a place of trust in the Lord. When the healing of memories starts from flashbacks, this is the surfacing of the wounded memory. When it is a childhood memory it is the child within crying out for healing. It is important to remember that where there is childhood trauma, very often there is the need for forgiveness which comes as one of the last stages of healing. This might also mean reaffirming the forgiveness that has already been released. This cleanses the wound that it may heal.

In our own prayer time, through listening prayer, we can enter into the presence of the Lord and ask Him to come and to heal that childhood memory or wound. The Father knows us. He is our creator. He knows everything about us: our complete history, present, and future. He is not bound by time. He knew us before we were even born, and He sees every influence upon our life. When there is a lack of love and compassion, especially as a child, then the child is starved of what is essential for his or her emotional and psychological well-being and growth. But Christ is there to bring healing. Healing the inner child will also bring healing to our bodies, hearts, and minds.

As we enter into the healing process, what is important is that one trusts. The child within must come to trust you, the adult. Now this may be hard if the child was wounded by a family member or a beloved and known adult. The child needs support from a person who will not be negative or anything like the oppressive adult. What is important is that as the child comes out of hiding he finds you, his adult, being supportive and there for him or her. You are there for the child's pain to come out and to come through. Christ is there with you holding both you and the child close; you can trust Him to work this out with you.

One of the main situations that can arise when we come to face our pain is that we can rationalise away the circumstance, like playing down the situation: *"Oh, it was years ago; I am okay now." "He or she was in a ba• moo•; they •i•n't really mean it."* Yes, this may be so, but whatever the reason, these events damaged you and truly wounded your being. We need to come out of any denial that can suffocate or repress our need for healing. It is also important for us to identify the wounds, call them by name, and not fear the reality or circumstance. It is with Christ that we walk upon the road of healing; we are not alone. However, we also bear in mind that whoever damages and wounds another is also a wounded person who has not been healed.

Judgement decisions

Another aspect is that of judgement decisions, that is, childhood vows. The Lord says, *"Do not ju*r*ge lest you will be ju*r*ge*r*."* We want justice and we know that as children, when we have been wronged, we may tend to lash out and make very strong and rash statements. Believe it or not, children are very justice-minded and will react as such. It is when dignity and self-worth have been damaged that children are not able to see the truth. As children we seek justice but know nothing of grace. We react and in our hearts we condemn, hold grudges and prejudices; we pass sentences; we dishonour and make vows against those who have caused us pain, even against ourselves. These vows often remain hidden, forgotten deep within our subconscious, but they are still active and have their effect.

Anger and resentment towards parents especially as growing teenagers cause tremendous damage to us when we, in turn, are parents and begin to parent our own children.

The Lord touches us and brings up the pains and situations or circumstances of these situations. We need to repent, forgive, and allow the Lord to heal those wounds and our thought patterns and allow Him to cleanse us, to set us free, to deliver us from all that binds and chains us to the past.

When we are dealing with a traumatic situation, whatever the situation, especially if harm has been done to us, sometimes the memory can be shocking and that, too, is necessary, for it releases grief. Anger then comes in, and this, too, is important for the healing of the inner child. Even if what happened was not intended but was accidental, the anger stirs up the truth that your person has been wounded. Whatever the circumstance you have been deeply wounded and this needs to stop here. Anger gives you the energy and impetus to take the steps that will not tolerate any further dysfunctional attitudes either around or within you, attitudes that may have dominated your life.

Betrayal

Betrayal is another deep wound especially when it is done by a family member or a close friend. The hurt and sadness begin to envelope us as we sense that betrayal. Dreams, hopes, and aspiration may have been ruined through this betrayal. What may be worse is what we believed to be true now turns out to be a lie. Our needs have not been met, and all that we had hoped or believed in comes crashing down like a pack of cards in the wind. But Christ is the one sure point. We must learn to lean on Him to help us through. He will never betray us. This is a big step to take, for even then we feel that He, too, will abandon and betray us. We project all our angers, disappointments, and betrayals onto Him. But we must, instead, give them to Him, give them to Him on the Cross that He, in turn, may heal and restore us.

Guilt and shame

Guilt and many times a sense of shame then sets in. This is false guilt and shame, for the child has done nothing wrong and this for sure must be dealt with. Jesus comes to heal our guilt and shame. The inner child is wounded and in pain because of what was done to him or her and not because of anything he or she had done.

However, even if the teen child has wilfully done wrong, the Lord still looks upon us as His broken children. Repentance and forgiveness of self and of others is an important stepping stone in our healing and walk towards restoration and wholeness.

The feelings of shame and loneliness can be devastating. We feel abandoned. We feel that we are bad, even unclean and this leads to a devastating loneliness, a separation from our adult self and others. It is very hard to allow these emotions to work themselves out from within us, but Christ is there with us. He took all our guilt and shame when He died on the Cross and gave us His Resurrection that we might rise with Him. When we come out on the other side, we then encounter and find our true self. When we hide our shame and pain from others, we are hiding it from ourselves. In acknowledging it, we come in touch with all that has been hidden and, in love, allow the Lord to heal us. In this way, we come in touch with our truest self, our true being.

If we have been wounded by our parents or family members know also that the wounded inner child may also represent several generations. Our parents may have also suffered during their own childhood and we carry within us the generational memory as well. In embracing the inner child, we are also embracing those generations of children within our family gone by who needed healing. Effects of woundedness and traumas can be transmitted through generations, for our parents and grandparents would not, may not have known of their inner child let alone how to allow Christ to heal the child within.

Forgiveness is essential to healing and the failure to give or receive forgiveness holds us in bondage to the wound and negative situation. Every time we forgive another, confess sin, and receive forgiveness we experience a healing of the wounds, of memories, and the cleansing of our hearts and consciences.

Jesus comes to set us free, to set the captives free from the chains that bind us, in this case, the chains caused by a childhood traumatic memory. We have the presence of Jesus with us. During this time of healing, we converse with the Lord, crying out to Him in our pain, anger, and frustration and allowing Him to deal with the situation. In so doing, we are allowing Him into those negative and embedded thought patterns, beliefs, and understanding which are to be exchanged for the truth received by listening to Jesus' healing and affirming Word, to His love, and to the Word of God found in the Scriptures. It is then that we can visualise Jesus speaking to us and ministering to our needs, to the inner child and us the adult. He wants to give us His peace and a deep sense of being loved. In so doing, Jesus is *'re-wiring or reformatting (a movern term)'* our being, establishing a new and fresh condition wherein God's truth is now spoken into our lives. As we pray in this way, the Spirit of the Lord enfolds us and makes us new. His truth now speaks to us and sets us free, for we are those who have received God's forgiveness and salvation. He is the source of the truth that will lead to healing. *"For the Spirit of truth will guive us into all the truth"* (John 16:13).

In the reading and praying of Scripture, the truth within gives us life for God's living Word is the double-edged sword that is 'alive and active.' He pours His Word of Life into our brokenness and His Word heals and changes us. His Word is active and effective, and it transforms our beliefs and changes us. All our negative imagery is then changed and transformed into symbols of goodness and light. We will have wholesome and biblical symbols as given to us in our Judeo-Christian heritage.

Visual imagery is also a powerful spiritual tool to the healing of the inner child. It gives peace about truth, and creates hope and direction for the next step of healing. People who picture God as strong, trustworthy, rescuing, and loving can often shorten their healing period.

The road to wholeness is unique for each person for it is the Lord who directs and counsels us for each step of the way. *"I wait patiently for the Lord; he turned to me and heard my cry. He lifted me out of the slimy pit, he set my feet upon a rock and gave me a firm place to stand. He put a new song in my mouth"* (Psalm 40:1-3). AMEN.

chapter eleven
the healing of
the mother wound

The first place of security of any living mammal, primarily us human beings, is our mother's womb. There the little one grows or should grow in the love, warmth, and nurturing of the mother. This is, sadly, not always the case.

As sons and daughters, our relationship with our mothers is one of the most significant in our lives, effecting how we see and view ourselves and our worth. Mother is there, a person who was to meet all our needs, first as a growing embryo in her womb, a neo-natal, then as an infant. She is there to help us develop into exploring toddlers, lively children, strong teens, and responsible adults. As children, our mothers were everything to us, yet we did not realise that they, too, had their limitations and very often their own brokenness was projected and transferred onto us from a very tender age, yes, even from conception. Through the womb we received all the emotions, heard their words, felt what was going on. As embryos, we could not rationalise the feelings, but we received them in our psyche and spirit. If our mothers rejected us, we would have felt deep rejection in our spirits. If she was inundated with fear, the little one felt it. If she was filled with joy, the little one felt it and rejoiced at being born. If she wanted to abort us then that fear becomes very real indeed.

Every emotion is felt and lived by the child in the womb. We are called to be set free from those very limitations that have been placed upon us without feeling guilty or ashamed. Many may feel the guilt, denial, or fear of actually admitting or verbalising their negative emotions, acknowledging the painful situations as a child, or that there were circumstances in the family that really wounded the little one. For many, the spiritual, psychological, and emotional umbilical cord has not been cut and as adults continue to live their lives tied to their mother, controlled by her fluctuating emotions. When we are still tied to our mothers in an unhealthy bond, we are unable to grow and become all that we are meant to be. Her inner voice of correction or control is still alive and loud in our hearts and minds. We cannot move in the freedom we would like. We may be aware of this, or maybe not, for we know and have lived nothing else, but the Lord calls us to be free in our own identity and not continue to live as an emotional, psychological extension of our mothers. The Lord wants us to have a true and healthy relationship with our mother and not an unhealthy bondage.

The Holy Spirit knows and has come to set us free. This is not a journey of accusation, but one of freeing, forgiving, and blessing our mothers in a way that we can be set free from the unhealthy ties which we have carried for far too long.

What was your relationship with your mother? Where do you automatically go when you think of her? Are your thoughts good or are you aroused to anger or feel pain and fear? What do you feel?

Our mothers were fundamental in our development as children, teenagers and young adults. They formed the very foundation of our emotional, psychological, and spiritual growth. In the patriarchal culture that has been with us for centuries, our mothers were often using dysfunctional coping mechanisms, whether they were emotional or psychological so they could cope with their everyday problems. This has affected both women and men.

When the mother has been steadfast and balanced, seeking God in a true and spiritual way, then the child feels safe and cherished and can grow well. There are examples of exemplary spiritual mothers and fathers like Mary's parents, Anna and Joachim. or woman/mother saints like Louis Martin and Marie-Azelie Guerin, parents of St. Theresa of Liseaux. Most mothers are good and balanced, wanting the best for their children. Many turn to their own wise mothers, seeking wisdom, care, and understanding in times of crisis to help understand the perceptions of life and feelings as we grow up, relate to others, and bring up our own children. It is natural and of God's right order that the son and daughter grow up and become their own persons.

Though our mothers may have done their best to nurture us, our lives have been laced with undercurrents of guilt, shame, control, and manipulations. We may even carry unresolved grief, disappointment, and resentment towards our mothers long into our adult lives. For men, this could so easily affect the way they subconsciously see their wives and relate to them. This deep pain is usually the result of unhealed core wounds that are passed on from generation to generation. It is here that we need Jesus and, indeed, Mary to come in to help us, to heal these areas of brokenness that still yearn for a mother's affirmation and love. We yearn for a nurturing that we have not received that we may live and be the person God has called us to be.

When we are affected with wounds, very often we can trace them to our childhood, to the way we would perceive ourselves, and this is very often through the eyes of our mother. Mother wounds, as in father wounds, are situations that would have formed into traumas, big or small, that more often than not, are passed down from generation to generation and have a profound bearing on our lives. When left unhealed, we pass on the wounds that our mothers and grandmothers before us failed to heal or bring to the Cross in repentance or healing. These wounds consist of toxic and oppressive beliefs, attitudes, words, ideals, perceptions, and choices. If we do not bring them up and out onto the Cross of Christ for healing, then we will pass them onto our children who will in turn repeat the cycle, harming their own children and their children's children with centuries of unresolved pain and brokenness creating deep traumas. We need to also acknowledge the pain we may have inflicted and passed onto our own children. Each person yearns for that deep recognition of mother and father – that yearning for love and acceptance.

The four fundamental functions of a mother are: to nurture, to protect, to empower, and to initiate. When those functions are lacking, the mother takes on a semblance and outer crust of care but is very distorted within. We have the arch types like the step mother in Cinderella, Snow White, and Rapunzel. These fairy tales tell us a lot. We see narcissism come to the fore and a cold and foreboding shadow of what a mother is meant to be.

Mothers and fathers relate in different ways to their children of the opposite sex. They play a critical role in establishing the social and emotional wave lengths. A mother with her daughter will teach her the strength of true womanhood, what it means to make decisions, to be strong, and allows her the freedom to grow and, yes, even to make mistakes. She teaches her the right attitude towards men, that is, if the mother has it herself. She shines forth the beauty of her womanhood and her self-worth. She allows her daughter to connect with herself to find out the joys and wonders of her womanhood. The mother with her son will show him the beauty of woman and what it means to be a gentleman that he, in turn, will seek to love his spouse in a way that is respectful and protective, giving his wife space to grow as her own person and his soul mate. A mother is a son's first connection to the feminine, and a father is a daughter's first connection to the masculine.

For sons, the mother wound can predispose boys to the murky aspects of the feminine, a moaning, emotionally controlling and manipulating woman. If he is not healed, there is a chance he could marry the same type of woman as his mother or hate women altogether. Many men also become culturally conditioned as boys to rely on the women with whom they are intimate to meet all (or at least most) of their deep emotional needs, which places an unrealistic burden on their future spouses for total emotional support. That is why it is vital for the son to have a strong relationship with the father who, in turn, is well balanced in his own masculinity. A woman wants to be a wife to her husband, not his mother; she wants to marry a man and not a boy! The husband wants his wife to be his wife, the woman by his side and his by hers, not a little girl sulking for every bauble expecting her husband to be like daddy responding to her every whim. They are to be in the partnership of the covenant of marriage, each complimenting the other.

Having said all of this, we must realise that we are all wounded and have our failings. However, we are all on a journey of grace, healing, restoration, and growth.

These are some indications of the effects of the mother wound:

- We may have low self-esteem which means having weak boundaries and are unable to say 'no.'. These could then lead to various forms of abuse. It may come across as being humble or serving, but it is a false humility which could then lead to rebellion. True serving comes from a free heart.

- We would have shame, which comes with low self-esteem. This would manifest itself in a deep core belief. You are looking into the mirror of self- hate and depreciation that has been presented to you as a child.

- We may be comparing ourselves to others continually walking in competition against others. Either wanting to have the upper hand or else putting ourselves down, we are never good enough. Others are rivals to you.

- We feel guilty and negative should anything good or some form of success come our way. The inner words of negation are forever speaking loudly into our heads and hearts. We should not have it! We do not deserve it!

- We are overly critical, not only self-critical, but we criticise everything and everyone. We are intolerable perfectionists and this is so that others see us as being perfect. This is a false mask that needs to be removed.

- The overly critical person has a constantly fault-finding attitude towards others and is unable to rejoice in what another may do or achieve. This person is at the very core of their being unable to accept or love their true self.

- Here the relationships working out of a subconscious mother wound have a high level of dependence, always wanting someone else's affirmation for their decisions or tasks. There is always the need to have someone to solve their problems and they could have a childish attitude towards life.

- There is the inability to speak up authentically and express your emotions fully for you may have received so much negative treatment from others as well as from your primary relationship with your mother.

- Then there is the victim/martyrdom attitude. The need to self-sacrifice when deep inside this is not real. Caring is superficial and there is the constant 'poor me, how good I am' attitude. There is no love or joy in this false giving. True sacrifice comes out of the freedom of the heart and sincere love even if it is a daily occurrence as in the caring for a sick person in the family. This type of caring is borne out of a deep love and respect even though one may be tired at times.

- The person always waits for the mother's permission even on the unconscious level to truly live life. They feel the need of mother's approval of any choice or decision even though the person may be a fully-grown adult. Some women and men still have their mothers choose their clothes for them as fully-grown adults. This does not mean one may not seek advice in the knowledge that you are given the freedom to discern and choose. In this way the relationship would be healthy.

- There could be conditions such as eating disorders, depressions, or even addictions.Moving away and detaching oneself from the mother as one grows up may not always be easy and is often strewn with difficulties.Moving away and detaching oneself from the clinging or possessive mother as one grows up is often fraught with struggles and outbursts. The problem would also lie where the son or daughter thinks differently from the mother because he or she is a different person and not an extension of the mother. He or she has not internalised her ideas or wave lengths. This could result in the outburst of mother's emotions and the child will suffer the mother's obvious disapproval, being made to feel that he or she is betraying the mother. The son or daughter does not want the possibility of losing the mother's love and approval, so internalising these limiting, unconscious beliefs is a form of loyalty and emotional survival for the son or daughter.

A mother can also and very directly be very jealous of her child and not help advance them into their future. She will use any form of control and manipulation to keep the son or daughter tied to them using health, emotions, any form so that the son or daughter will not have a life of their own. Should the son or daughter try to move out of this cobweb, this will trigger instant reactions. The compassion and desire to please the mother comes out of carrying and being responsible for the mother's emotions, even if this causes deep inner conflict with the sense that it is better to remain hidden than to move out and be my own person.

Each person has in one form or another felt partly to be blamed for the mother's pain. Why? As a child we do not understand the emotions within the family unit even though we feel it. This is where our guilt and brokenness lie. The mother would say, *"Eat your foo* to make mummy happy."* Or *"Be a goo* girl or boy because mummy is not well."* Or *"Mummy is happy if you *o this or the other*!"* This is always inferring that there is pain if the opposite is done. If I do not eat my food, if I do not obey, if I do not do what she wants then this will bring her displeasure and she will not speak to me, she will punish me, etc. Mothers who use emotions to bring their children to obey them and do what they want are creating mother wounds if this is persisted and not balanced out with positive mothering. If we do not address this unconscious belief, as an adult we will still be walking around with it, greatly limiting ourselves.

If we do not tackle the mother wound, then we will carry it with us throughout our lives for it is present in our everyday problems, habits, and situations. If we avoid dealing with the pain associated with one of the most primary and foundational relationships in our lives, we are missing a crucial opportunity to discover the truth of who we are and to authentically and joyfully live that truth.

However, we are not responsible for the well-being of our mother's emotions, and this is important, for we may hear the words from the inner voice moaning of her self-sacrifice; therefore, you are to sacrifice your life for her now;.it would be selfish to move on to achieve my dream in life if my mother could not achieve hers; to tend to her emotions means loyalty and not rejection.

These thought patterns and words continue to feed the mother wound. This negative attitude is one of selfishness, narcissism, and jealousy. The truth is, a mother wants her children to achieve more and beyond what she achieved. If a mother has not dealt with her own pain or disappointments or come to terms with the sacrifices she has had to make, then the nurturing of her son or daughter may be underlined with suggestions that subtly inject shame, guilt, or obligation. They can seep out in the most ordinary situations, usually in some form of criticism or some form of bringing praise back to the mother. *"If it were not for me you woul. not have .one this, or ha. that, or succee.e. in this job, etc."* It may not be the words themselves, but rather the tone and attitude with which it is conveyed that can carry hidden resentment.

If the son or daughter fears reaching their potential and senses that the mother feels threatened or abandoned should he or she strive for their own dreams and ambitions, then you are operating out of the mother wound. Should the son or daughter feel the mother's envy and anger even though this may never have been verbalised, that deep feeling that I cannot move out, then you are functioning out of the mother wound. No amount of self-sacrifice can save the mother who, in turn, needs her own healing. On the contrary, it will only feed that deep hole within her which she is trying to fill by living her life through you. In many instances, we can liken this to a form of parasite love. The mother wants her son or daughter to be a continuation of her life and will live her life out in them. This is all wrong and most certainly not of God.

The best thing is for the son or daughter to find themselves in their healing and to cut the negative umbilical cords, and, if necessary, get away or at least keep a distance for a while. It is only then that the mother can in her floundering, find the place of true healing. Being loyal to one's mother is not feeding her wounds but allowing her to come out, even though it is painful, into the light of truth. Stand up for yourself if need be. As an adult, love your mother but be firm in love and move on and out of her controlling and manipulative web. If we do not, we will only make it worse for ourselves and make the situation worse all around. If there are serious issues with the mother, that is, sickness, then that, too, has to be dealt with in a very discerning manner. Sick people can be very good manipulators especially if they have been controlling throughout their lives.

Motherhood is not easy and no mother is a super-mum! Mothers can go through a lot of true sacrifices for their children and many are happy to do so especially when they see their children moving forward in their lives.

We must not cling to this dream of an ideal and perfect mother. We are all human with our failings and mistakes. If a mother has in her own life not received love, she then would not be able to give love in return. We cannot give what we do not have. It is not your responsibility to change your mother, but you are called to love her. If you yearn for true motherhood, then turn to the motherhood of God. We also find this motherhood in Mary when Jesus gave her to us on the Cross. We may have to grieve the loss and absence of a mother. She may have been physically present but not been there nurturing, or been there to walk with you as you grew up. Many persons have had to grow up alone even though their mothers were present in the home.

You are allowed to grieve the pain of this loss as this helps with the healing. This takes time, often years, but eventually we look upon our mothers with love, tenderness, and understanding in compassion. If there is anger, this needs to be processed properly. We bring all our pain and anger to the Cross of Christ.

Unfortunately, society today is not good towards the mother. She often needs to work and also look after a family.

The sacrifices are enormous and stressful and can lead to built-up anger. If the mother does not find help and deal with her internal issues, then she will vent them onto her children. She needs to grieve her loss, and yes, maybe she had to give up a promotion to be at home more with the children. Yes, maybe her choice of husband was not the ideal. Maybe the first child was conceived out of wedlock and she married the father of the child out of pressure or necessity because she was young. So many questions and pains and losses. If these are not dealt with then the wounds are passed on and the suffering increases. The children must never be made to feel responsible for the mother's or father's mistakes. That was their responsibility and theirs alone. Now they are to care for the children and bring them up as best as possible in the love and nurturing owed them.

Mothers and fathers are not perfect. They, too, are human and have a lot to deal with. There will be disagreements; that's normal. There will be things said, but we must to ready to ask forgiveness and to forgive. When the mother wound is being healed there will be a true sense of being and life. The Lord comes and restores you to wholeness and calls you by name. It is in the healing that we can come to strong and true communication one with the other.

The healing of the mother wound is not about your mother but about you. It is being set free to discover who you truly are. You are being born again out of the womb into new life. The umbilical cord is cut and you can now live a life that is all yours. You are free to love your mother in the best way possible—free to truly love, to say 'yes' and to say 'no!' We do not feel responsible for our mother's pain knowing that the Lord will help her to deal with it, and the link of her projection and transference is being severed. But we are very much asked to forgive and to pray for our mothers.

As new beings healed from the mother wound, we are more confident and skilled in handling our emotions seeing them as a source of wisdom and learned information. We have healthy boundaries that support the coming out of our uppermost and true self. We develop a solid inner adult that provides unconditional love, support, and comfort to your inner child. It is knowing yourself as competent, feeling that anything is possible, open to the wonder of becoming, and able to receive all good things from the Lord. It is being in constant contact with your inner goodness and knowing your good traits, and yes, even your failings, but these are yours and not those superimposed from your mother. It is joy in the ability to bring your true self into everything you do as you make your own right decisions and discernment. It is having deep compassion for yourself and other people, with a good sense of humour. It is no longer needing external affirmation for all you do. It is no longer needing to prove yourself to others but to go forward because you believe in it. It is feeling safe as you are and having a freedom to be yourself, to grow and to become all that you are meant to be. We no longer carry the burden of our mother's pain seeing ourselves as unimportant. We can now have compassion for our mothers and pray for them without becoming entangled in their cobwebs.

We can confidently commence and move forward into our own lives, with the energy and vitality to create what we desire without shame or guilt, but with passion, power, joy, confidence, and love.

chapter twelve

the healing of
the father wound

The father wound is a wound that is embedded deeply in the heart and soul of the wounded one. It is not a wound that lies on the surface but effects the very substance of the broken person.

In the depths of the human person, there is a craving deep within for that intimate connection with others, but we are often left without the tools for creating these loving, nurturing relationships. A big reason for this has to do with the primary role fathers typically play in families. Rather than nurturing their sons and daughters or developing intimacy with them, fathers often spend the majority of their time enforcing the rules and discipline of the home, or working, or else he is an absent father.

Human fatherhood is meant to image the Fatherhood of God and bring harmony, strength, protection, and love into the family. The wife and children need to feel loved and secure in the loving environment the father provides. His role is not to just provide and see to the material needs of the family, but also see to the emotional, psychological, and spiritual welfare of the family. He is the one responsible and answerable before God for what happens in the family and how its members are being formed. The Spirit in Paul in Ephesians 5:25, 28 has spoken out very clearly of the role of the husband and thus fathers in the family: *"Husbands, love your wives, just as Christ loves the Church and gave himself up for her in order to make her holy... in the same way husbands should love their wives as they do their own bodies. He who loves his wife loves himself."* In Ephesians 6:4, we read, *"Fathers do not provoke your children to anger, but bring them up in the discipline and instruction of the Lord."*

God the Father created us to be awakened and formed by our fathers. The father calls out the son into manhood and calls out the daughter into womanhood. In many situations, unfortunately, the father was either distant and silent, rather like a shadow, the absent father in the family. Or else he was aggressive and domineering, a sergeant major of discipline, or very much the patriarch, stoical, where the whole family's life is centred upon his needs and wants. True bonding never really took place and the child, be it a boy or girl, is left without the father's protective pillar of strength, the strong fatherhood and manhood role model in his or her life. The reality is, if this father wound is not healed, it is very hard to have proper relationships with others, with those in authority, fermenting a seething rebellion. There could be confusion in relationships between the sexes. It would also then be very hard to have a true relationship with God the Father and to some extent the Lord Jesus Christ.

More often than not if there is the failure to experience affection and praise from a father this can result in sadness, anger, lack of self-confidence, anxiety or mistrust that can emerge at any stage later on in life. This situation, if not resolved before marriage, can continue into marriage affecting the spouse and once again the children. For example: married couples can experience unhappiness because the childhood sadness has never been resolved and is unconsciously misdirected with anger, contempt, and often viciousness towards one's spouse. This conflict has contributed to the present breakdown in marriages and families creating the divorce and separation culture.

We have already spoken about forgiveness, so we now understand how important it is that we forgive our fathers for past hurts. It is also helpful to correct him respectfully if he is doing something in the present that is painful. We are to honour our father for that is a command of the Lord. Even if, for one reason or another, we cannot have a relationship with our father, we still need to honour him in our hearts. At the same time, it can be valuable to ask a father for forgiveness for the times when we may have hurt him.

It is also significant to also try to see the goodness in the fathers and to be loyal to that goodness, then try to understand the different problems in a father's life and to think about forgiving him for his weaknesses. Without forgiveness, one remains a prisoner of one's past, locked in a place of bitterness and resentment. Also, it is important to remember that in particular, a man cannot harbor resentment toward his father and then have a healthy male confidence because men are often modeled after their father. In addition, unresolved anger with a father increases the likelihood of repeating his weaknesses, but not his strengths. In the respect of a daughter, there is also the chance that the daughter will marry someone like her own father if her anger and resentment towards her father is not forgiven and dealt with.

Each child comes into the world dependent upon their parents to be loved, taken care of, accepted, found worthy, and be blessed. The father wound is the absence of this love from the father. When we are talking about the father, we are referring to the father who has 'fathered' the child, that is, the natural father or the father figure in the family.

The wounds inflicted are several and are caused by:

- Neglect: This tells me that I am unimportant and not worth it. Neglect can be experienced in different areas of life: physical, emotional, psychological. This can then lead to emotional and psychological abandonment.

- Absence: Divorce, separation, death, or not being present in their lives. The absent father is not there for family events, not there for school events and for the basic fatherly nurturing of the child. The absent father can be at home physically but not be there emotionally and does not show any form of interest in the children. As we said, he is like a shadow in the home.

- Abuse: Mental, physical, sexual, spiritual. This kind of aggressive behaviour is very destructive and does cause enormous damage.

- Control: Oppressive domination, overly disciplined. This ferments deep anger and a repressive aggression.

- Withholding love, blessings and or affirmations. These are deficiencies that lead to a profound lack of self-acceptance and deep rejection.

- Spiritual and religious manipulation and oppression that distorts the Father-love of God.

The effect of a father wound is low self-esteem, a deep emotional pain inside and more often than not a performance orientation that makes us "doers" rather than "being." When this wound is addressed, we need to overcome the various obstacles that have been put up, for the defence mechanism is very much in place. We tend to have four barriers that inhibit the healing of this wound:

- The wound itself – Continuous deep emotional hurt inside and very often a deep confusion of who I am. This can also lead to gender confusion.

- Lies – We believe the lies about ourselves and can even accept the lies and deceptions of peers to be accepted. There are deep misconceptions about the self, be it emotional, psychological, sexual, and spiritual and about what it means to be a father and a person. We have no understanding of what fatherhood means either from our natural father or God the Father.

- Fear –There may be no will to confront or change, and the person would rather live the lie than face the tsunami wound within. They believe the "I'm alright" stance. "I can manage."

- Sin – The person could be locked in a deep-seated anger that refuses to acknowledge any form of forgiveness towards the father. This causes pride which is a blocked will that neither seeks to confess sin or receive forgiveness.

When we hold a conception of our father as angry, violent, uncaring, indifferent, distant/withdrawn, absent/abandoning, alcoholic, condemning and/or critical, we tend to believe the following words about ourselves:

I am unworthy; I am stupid; I am incompetent; I am unloved or unlovable.

As long as we accept these words *as truth*, we will experience depression, anxiety, and anger, living our lives under this dark cloud and respond aggressively or very coldly towards others.

When the father is unemotional, rather stoical, he sets barriers to any form of demonstration of feelings in the family and sets high and often unreachable expectations from the wife and children. The children never seem to make it in their father's eyes. The father has never been proud of them or ever affirmed their aspirations or endeavours, let alone help them in their discouragement or failings.

Then we have the mysognist father for whom the girl is but a mere object and totally incapable of anything, especially if it is academic, careerwise, etc. and for him the boy is put on a pedestal. Unfortunately, this sets the stage for further sin in the family. The girl will very likely marry a mysognist or become full of hatred and contempt for men that she could become misandrous, and the boy himself will follow his father's footsteps.

An important time for both girls and boys is their leap into womanhood and manhood. Here the father plays an important role. He defines the girl as being a woman like her mother. He is proud of her; she is as pretty and lovely as he remembers her mother. He is protective of the boys around her and smiles and coos when she looks pretty in her dresses. The girl feels precious and worth it. Her father is the first man in her life, and his attitude towards her sets the stage and direction of how she is to expect boys and men to treat her.

The boy growing into puberty will have so many physical reactions. He needs to not only have a father but a friend to be with him, to steer him into manhood, to show him how to be strong and protective, how to stand firm in trails, and how to express himself. The father's affirmation is vital for the young man's feelings of inadequacy. Some may have witnessed distortions of true manhood that has deeply wounded them. Some of the deepest wounds lie in these feelings of inadequacy, which can then poison other relationships and make true intimacy difficult. Men who grew up with fathers they were unable to please often carry around a suffocating belief system. Because so many boys do not have a father affirming their leap into manhood, that transition is often filled with feelings of fear, anger, and frustration instead of confidence and security. Lonely and discouraged boys become isolated and alienated men. In this isolated state, men continue to desire closeness and connection, but they often have no notion of how to achieve it.

It is because of this predicament that many men seek out sexual fantasy in an attempt to find some sense of intimacy. Many men feel a void in their lives, often created by the wounds of the past, and some men attempt to fill that void with illicit sexual activities. Men's desire for intimacy and connection is real, powerful, and appropriate. But when men try to satisfy that desire in the form of sexual fantasies and acts, they find merely illusions or shadows of true relationship and connection. These kinds of sexual fantasies take them into a deeper dark bondage and sin.

When this happens we would have a hard and difficult time to relate or even turn to God the Father. We would project our natural father's image onto God the Father. The child's understanding of God the Father is infected by the personal experience he or she has with the natural father. When misconceptions about God are present (that He is angry, judgmental, unhappy with me, fearsome, legalistic, quick to punish and slow to forgive) we then believe that we cannot be acceptable or lovable to the Father. We may be told that God is love, but yes, He loves everyone but me. Or He may love tolerate me, but He cannot possibly like me. The lies in our hearts and minds tell us that I am not good enough. If I am not lovable, it is my fault; therefore, I am guilty and ashamed and because of this I must try my best, wear a mask if necessary, and prove that I can do it. I must work harder to justify myself so that I will be loved and accepted.

As long as we accept these words as truth, we will seek to perform and prove our worth through perfectionism and materialism, or seek addictions to cover up the pain.

Healing

It is only through the love and heart of Jesus Christ, in the power of the Holy Spirit that we can enter and heal this devastating father wound. God the Father is perfect and reliable, unlike the human father for "*the Lord is near to the brokenhearted and saves the crushed in spirit*" (Psalm 34:18). Also in Psalm 147:3, "*the Lord heals the brokenhearted, binds up their wounds.*"

However, a healing balm for men and women who suffer from the father wound is through the Word of God, obtaining a biblical understanding of what a father truly is, and through a relationship with Jesus Christ. Both men and women can begin to experience healing. More healing can occur through accountability and community with other Christian brothers and sisters. It is in the developing of healthy Christian relationships with others who are truly present, and experiencing a loving relationship through the Holy Spirit in Jesus Christ with our eternal Father who is always present, that we find we can share our wounds with fellow travelers. The journey itself can provide tremendous healing. It is in coming out of our own woundedness and brokenness that we can most clearly see the vital nature of our relationship with Christ and others.

When we address the father wound, we do it with the knowledge and understanding of the heart of God the Father. This Father whom through Jesus we can call 'Abba' is close to us. Jesus is the one who takes us to the Father as we invite Him into our wounds created by our natural fathers. Through Him and in the healing of memories, emotions, and deep psychological wounds, we very slowly begin to recognise the truth about one's self as a child of God. We see ourselves as truly being loved and wanted by the Father. He not only loves us.H He likes us. He is proud of us. He affirms us. This takes time and more often than not alot of pain. We begin to touch the heart of God and allow His heart and love to touch and heal ours.Like the parable of the prodigal son, we then see how much we are loved unconditionally not matter the mistakes we may have made because of our brokenness. Not only that, but God the Father also loves our natural father and through this love we begin to find the strength and will to forgive our natural father. In 1 John 4:19, we are told *"We love because he love, us first."* We see ourselves as His beloved creation beautifully and wonderfully made, freed from the chains of sin and all that can bind us to the darkness. Jesus whose blood sets us free is there for us, for it is in Him that we have been set free. First Peter 2:24 says, *"By His woun,s you have been heale,."*

As we invite Jesus into those painful memories and deep-seated angers, He begins to change us. We see the differences of character from Jesus to our natural father, and slowly through the Holy Spirit, we begin to gravitate towards Jesus and God the Father, turning to Him as our true Father.

As we invite Jesus into the wounds created by our natural father, we ask Him to heal specific memories, to cleanse us from words that we have carried embedded in our hearts and minds, always sending out those devastating echoes into our life. These words have been held onto for so long that they have formed us. We ask to be released from the control and domination of attitudes that have formed us telling us that we are incapable and unlovable. This is not who we truly are. Attitudes and words that we had accepted as the truth are not who we truly are. As we enter into the place of healing, we allow the Spirit to speak the truth of who we truly are, how He sees us, and who we are to Him. In so doing, we make the decision to release forgiveness to our natural father and to cut all the negative bonds, all the negativity that we have received from him: the hurtful words, the actions, the pain, his lack of attention, not being loving or present, not blessing us, affecting negatively our image of God the Father. We make a decision to repent for having accepted and believed and lived out of the lies said about us, for God the Father is telling us that we are different, beautifully and wonderfully made, made in His image and likeness to be a joy to Him and to have confidence in ourselves and the work of our hands. We renounce all the negativity we have received as truth in our lives, even the lies we have said about ourselves as a consequence of our brokenness.

We then reject the false self we have lived out of and enter into our true identity as a child, son or daughter, of the Father. We enter and take the blessings that are ours through being a child of the Father, entering into our inheritance that is there for us in Christ Jesus.

We receive the Father's words of truth that I am loved and lovable, I am accepted, I am chosen, I am God's child, I am God's creation. He will never leave or forsake me. I am forgiven and I have an inheritance that is mine, and now, nothing can separate me from the love of God found for me in Christ Jesus.

Accept yourself as a child of God.

As we understand the truth about God's love and come to know our true self in Christ, it will free us to let go of the pain and forgive our natural father. This new perspective created in us will now enable us to see our natural father through different eyes and allow us to live in freedom. Then another miracle can occur. Going through this healing, our natural father is being healed for through our releasing of forgivness, he is receiving the blessings that were his also. He, too, has suffered and we leave this healing into the Lord's hands. Because the Lord has asked us in the Commandments to honour our father and mother, we release forgiveness and bless our father knowing his weakness and fraility. We trust in God the Father, who is also his Father, to have mercy and compassion. For with the same love and mercy we have received, we want our father to receive the same.

To honour our father and mother is the only commandment that brings with it a blessing: *"Honour your father an• your mother, that your •ays may be long in the lan• which the Lor• your Go• gives you"* (Exodus 20:12).

chapter thirteen
from the wounded child to a true image in Christ

We have spoken of the suffering inner child, yet in truth we are all God's children and we look to Him as Father. As human beings we have suffered in the various stages of our lives. Created in God's image and likeness our woundedness and sin has distorted that image and in so doing our self-image has been broken.

Factors that make up our self-image

There are four source or factors that create or construct our self-image and these are built into us in our early years and continue into our life time if not dealt with. This is why the inner child needs healing especially when there is a wrong self-image. The inner woundedness is caused by the world outside of us, the inner world which is the way the child perceives things deep inside which includes Satan and his evil and God's Word.

Our outer world includes all the factors that have gone into our make-up:family, birth, infancy, childhood, upbringing, schooling, teen years, life around us, and even the way we relate to others. This happens because of the world around us. This can mean any sort of emotional, psychological, sexual, and or physical abuse. Our experience of the outer world includes how we are treated at home and in school as well as by those in authority which also includes Church, teachers, family, etc. Also, the way we were taught to behave as children whether in a confident but polite manner or whether we were subdued and taught that children were seen and not heard is how we eventually relate to people and things in the world which are continuously being thrown at us. The world has a voice of its own that is clamouring for attention, and unless we have a well-formed, strong, and healthy inner child we can easily fall into the mindset and voice pattern of the world.

As a child does not have the reasoning capacity or understanding of an adult, the child needs to be nurtured not only as a person but also spiritually if he or she is to grow into the full stature of a true human being in the identity of God. St. Paul speaks of a child's attitudes in 1 Corinthians 13:9-12. A child only knows things partially. The child feels and senses but does not know or understand. The child is bombarded with images of who and what they are and should be. This is done in a way that the child ends up looking like one of those images in the hall of mirrors of an amusement fair. What are the mirrors saying? This is what happens to us: we become distorted and out of proportion. We begin to believe what these mirrors are telling us. When the child is bombarded with these definite mirror images it is then that the child develops the image of him or herself. We are affected by the way we have been related to as a child.

A father returns from home, just nods at the children and wants to rest. He is not thinking of anything wrong or that he is doing anything wrong; he only wants to rest. He is not giving his attention to the child. But what message does that give to the child? The child may then begin to feel unwanted, uncared for. Does that mean that the father truly does not care for the child? Not at all, but that is the impression and image the child is receiving. We then begin to talk and relate out of this image. The child then becomes a person pleaser trying to please everyone, and the character and personality becomes distorted as it cannot find its true self.

Like in the hall of mirrors the person begins to change and distort depending on which situation he finds himself in, instead of having a firm foundation in Christ and being able to adapt to each situation without compromising his true self and identity. If there are real problems and the family is dysfunctional then the child can truly become hurt and distorted. We must remember that a child does not know how to express himself in a comprehensive manner. Children do not tell the mother or father you hurt me with your words. They cannot understand things to that depth, but they do feel emotions which they cannot understood let alone expressed. So, they react since that is all they know. They shout, break things, misbehave, etc. There will be dysfunctional behaviour of some kind. Because each child is different, they will find different ways and means to gain attention. This can continue even when grown up and is an adult. This does not stop, for the inner child is still in there clamouring for attention and knocking for help. We can suppress the hurt or ignore the child within but this does not mean that the child is not there.

God wants to heal us and give to each and every one of us our true God-given identity.

You are a child of God

Do you know that you are a child of God? Do you know it in your heart? The physical stretch from the top of our heads, therefore our minds to our hearts is about 40cm. That's not very far, but the journey from the mind to the heart is a very long journey. We need to know our identity in our hearts. We are the children of the Father. For those who have been deeply wounded by their natural fathers, even the term father may upset you.

We have a God-given identity. Whatever your name, you are you; there is no one else like you. Think of the time from Adam and Eve to now: all the billions of people from the very beginning of humanity and those still yet to come, still there will never, ever be someone like you. You are so unique. If you are made in the image of the Father then can you imagine what God is like. Isn't it amazing. If each person on this earth is a reflection of God, for we are made in the image and likeness of God and as baptised persons have God inside us, do we not know and realise the enormity of this wonder and mystery. This is the Holy Spirit, who is not a bird, but a person living inside of us, giving us Christian identity, and making us children of the Father. Baptism is one of the greatest gifts we have been given.

As children we have developed the image of ourselves just like that mirror. The child begins to talk, act, and relate to people in a way that would have been appropriate to the picture of those mirrors. If there are problems in the family then we become distorted and our inner child becomes hurt. In this, hurt we learn to suppress and slowly we ignore the child within. This does not mean that the child is not there, but slowly our true God-given identity is being suppressed, and we begin to suppress our feelings and emotions and are being psychologically wounded.

The distorted image of God is reflected within us

Our distortion of the image of God within us starts when we are young. We may also have a distorted image of who God the Father is. In our life at home, was God shown as love or a judgemental tyrant? These are attitudes that reflect God to us. We project the characters, attitudes, and personalities of our earthly parents and those in authority onto God. We then begin to feel who God the Father is when we are formed in this way, for we become bent and distorted and then we fail to listen to God properly in the fullness of our being. We fail to accept ourselves and this creates a barrier to wholeness in Christ.

Sadly, we do not listen aright either, for what is said is understood and translated into warped thought patterns. If a mother is busy and cannot play with her child then the child could inadvertently misunderstand the mother and take on board the feeling that mother does not have time for her, meaning that she is not worth the time, thus meaning she is not worth it! So, in fact how do we act and speak as adults and parents? Is it our inner child speaking? Are we projecting our own broken and wounded childhood onto our children? For what we say is so often mirrored onto our children. Then the other distortion is when we are very sugary in our approach in a way that we can spoil our children and not allow Godly discipline to create strong and safe borders for them. Or are we sugary to adults in such a way and so much so that the person feels humiliated? Flattery is not healthy as it reveals a very insincere attitude and can be and is very often manipulative. Flattery is also born out of an inner need to be recognised and appreciated. It has, as a foundation, a servile attitude which needs to idolise another human being. This needs healing for we are to have a healthy approach to one another, to hold no one in idolatry, and worship and serve the Lord alone.

When there is no sincerity or truth, when there is a hidden coldness or rejection in an adult, the child within can feel and sense these things but cannot express them properly. The child can feel and sense when something is not right but is unable to process his or her feelings into reason and so take action. Therefore, what results are unbalanced emotional reactions and expressions from the child which are often then dealt with by the adult in a disciplinary manner instead of the adult trying to understand what is happening to the child. The child feels unable to express himself and the more this happens the more the child feels suppressed and goes into repression and anger. We need to communicate and listen to the child, appreciate what he or she is saying and then speak. We need to nurture and speak truth, exercise Godly discipline where necessary but create a sound, healthy and a loving place for the child to grow. As we do this, our own inner child is also being healed for the Lord touches and heals us in our deepest places.

In the expression of the term child, we understand this on two levels: the inner child within us and our relationship with the Father as His child (the child of the Father). The child within is always growing up but is always the child. The trouble is, we are adults who have lost the childhood wonder. Do you feel excited at Christmas? That is the child in you. The lights, the Christmas tree, the crib—do those excite you? That is the child in you.

God the Father is building up a child so that the child can reflect His image and likeness within him. Yet life and its evil want to throw everything it has to destroy the image of God in the child. That is Satan's primary goal: to destroy our identity.

In the Genesis account of Adam and Eve, the first sin (disobedience) immediately brought distortion to their identity which was questioned by Satan in the form of a serpent: *"Di♦ Go♦ tell you?"* It was there that Satan began to separate man from his identity in God. As his identity was one with God he could walk with God in obedience, but when the identity is destroyed man then walks in disobedience. Satan wants you to take on another identity and that identity is not of God. In the temptations of Jesus in the desert, the evil one told Jesus in the form of a subtle question *"if you are the son of Go♦ then...?"* He was questioning Jesus' identity. When Jesus was on the cross, Satan speaking through the Pharisees told Him *"f you are the Son of Go♦, come ♦own from the cross."* He struck at Jesus' identity. The evil one wants to destroy your identity.

St. Paul tells us in 1 Corinthians 6:19 that we are the temples of the Holy Spirit. *"Do you not know that your body is a temple of the Holy Spirit within you, which you have from God."* This is the image of God in the child. That is why self-image and identity are important. In each one of us there are the effects of original sin. Baptism removes original sin but we still suffer the effects from the original sin, for we are of a fallen nature and the pressures of life are going to affect us. We do not just receive wounds, but we hurt and wound others too. We need to repent and ask forgiveness. Satan uses our own words to increase our brokenness, putting salt into a wound, and as the accuser, points his finger in heinous accusation: *'You did that! Do you think you are good?'*

There is a constant barrage of accusations. Satan is a liar, the accuser, the deceiver who deceives and distorts everything for his own purpose, and his primary purpose is our destruction. He thought he had killed Jesus and gleefully rubbed his hands, but Jesus said, *"It is finished and into your hands I commend my spirit"* (Luke 23:46). Jesus was obedient unto death and at that point, evil was destroyed. The Resurrection was the fulfilment of all His obedience for the Lord obeyed the Father to the Cross. Evil could not destroy Christ. Death could not hold Him and He rose from the dead.

All the work of the Cross and the glory of the Resurrection is for each and every one of us. At Baptism we are baptised into the Cross and Resurrection of our Lord Jesus, and His Cross is at work in your life, so that whatever you are going through the Lord will bring to Resurrection. *"What evil has purpose, for our ,estruction the Lor, will bring to the goo,"* (Genesis 50:20). The evil one presses on our inferiority, on our fears and lack of self-worth, and on all those diseased emotions that affect us, constantly hitting our wounds.

Repentance and forgiveness

No two persons are alike. We know that our children are not alike and we are not alike as brothers or sisters. But we all have our physical, emotional, and spiritual characters and capacities which we bring into the world and the lives around us. Within each person there is the effect of original sin for none of us came into the world neutral. Things are going to affect us. We are not just receivers of wounds, but we, too, hurt and wound others. Therefore, we also carry this responsibility to repentance and ask for forgiveness. Another aspect is Satan, who is a liar, uses our words, our brokenness to damage us even further. He presses on the wounds so that our feelings of inferiority, fear, anger, lack of self-worth and all our diseased emotions are heightened and take over our lives.

Because of this we need to stand firm and take responsibility for our actions and words as this closes the door in Satan's face. He wants to prevent our healing and especially of us trying to get to the root of all our pain. He has been defeated by the Cross of Christ and so does not want the Cross of Christ to have effect in our lives.

Distorted image of God

Another point that may need healing and usually does is the concept and image we have of God. We are moving from a low self-image to a totally new identity in Christ—a Christian self-image. We have to know the true image of God. It is only God and His Word that speaks truth to us. In the world, there are many philosophies and we live in a time of relativism. I like it; it doesn't hurt anybody so I will do it. This has brought so much destruction. What is the image we have of God? Is He a Father Christmas, a judge, a Zeus? Can you speak to God? We know He is spirit. He is father and mother so how can we approach Him? Jesus said, "Whoever has seen me has seen the Father" (John 14:8-10). We have seen Jesus. At least we know Him through the Word, and we experience Him in our hearts.

Do we read and pray the Word of God? We eat food every day, don't we? The Word of God is food for our mind and our heart. How can we know ourselves and the Father if we do not pray the Word every day? St. Jerome said that *'the ignorance of Scripture is the ignorance of Christ.'* We may have been taught as children many warped things about God through stories and ideas which are simply not theologically correct. There are also distortions of God that have come from well-meaning priests or religious stemming from their attitudes and wrong teaching of the Gospel. Coupled with, maybe dysfunctional parenting we have a very wrong image of God. We think that God wants to humiliate and belittle us, wants us to suffer and enjoys our suffering. Many of us have been shattered and have the distorted image of what it means when Jesus said we are *"to carry the cross"* since this has been given such wrong and distorted theological meanings. Jesus suffered that we could be free and healed; otherwise, why go to doctors, psychologists, and psychiatrists to be healed? In our suffering, He is there with us and our suffering becomes redemptive suffering until it is healed. God does not gloat over our suffering. Christian humility is not to destroy and belittle, but it is to know the truth.

chapter fourteen

wrong submission / right submission leads to obedience in Christ

"Love ,oes not consist of gazing at each other, but in looking outwar,
together in the same ,irection."

— Antoine de Saint-Exupéry, "Airman's Odyssey"

In our early childhood, we learned in our catechism the very basic reasons of what we were created for: *"Go, ma,e me to know Him, to love Him, an, to serve Him in this worl,, an, to be happy with Him for ever in Heaven."* However, the reality in our lives, as we know, is very different. From the fall of Adam and

Eve, man and woman no longer look straight up to the Father but are bent one towards the other. We are bent to material things, to ideals, philosophies, careers, even those things that are good like our work or families or even hobbies. We do not put God the Father first in our lives. We do not look straight up to Him. What does *'to be bent'* mean? We all know what it means to bend down. To be bent means to lean in that bending position towards another, or something else. That bent posture is the position of worship. If we can imagine that, we will realise what is being said. We only worship God, no one and nothing else. When we stand upright, we look up to God, our face in full exposure to Him. In the Greek, upright is *Akokos*. This means upright and innocent, without deception, whereas evil is *Kakos*. Philosophy says that ignorance creates a void that leaves room for evil; ignorance leaves a door open to deceit. In Hosea 4:6, the Lord cries out *"my people perish, are ᵻestroyeᵻ for lack of knowleᵻge."*

The very meaning and purpose in our lives is to live in communion with God, in humble submission and obedience to Him not as a master, but as one who calls us into His love, as one who has made us and calls us into being. Christ came to restore all that has been broken and to bring us back into communion, into right submission and obedience to the Father and thus into right relationship one with the other.

We have, through the Fall, been separated from the presence of God. We have fallen into the consciousness of self or the consciousness of the other. This is sin and makes us incomplete. The fallen self is turned inwards. We are selfish with misconceived feelings and attitudes. We cannot listen to God properly, and we are more likely to be people pleasers than God pleasers. We live off the *"respect of man an* not the *love of, or love for Go* which in turn *oes not allow us to love our neighbour as we shoul*."* Christ is not the centre of our lives.

The cart wheel

Let us give an example of a cart wheel with Christ as the centre, that is, the axle. The spokes go out from the centre of the wheel, the axle to the outer ring. Each spoke represents either a person, activity, friends, or family in our lives. For the wheel to turn properly the axle in the centre must be well balanced, if not, the wheel will not only not turn but will break. The spoke is not the centre of the wheel; the axle is the centre. This is the same with us. If we live from the spokes, if we make the spokes the centre and not the axle, we cannot function as we should.

To live from the spokes means that we live solely for our work, our hobbies, career, friends, even family without looking to Christ and for His will. When we do this then the wheel will not turn properly. Christ shows us how to love properly. This is the first commandment: *"to love the Lord with all our heart, mind and strength and to have no other God but him."* Imagine living from one of the spokes—doing only what the children want, what my husband or wife wants, what my colleagues at work want, what society wants—without giving a thought to what the Lord says in the situation, or what He would want. Is that not wrong submission? Sometimes we would have to take a stand, yes, even against our husbands, or our wives, or other family member and not go along with what is happening. This is what being bent is. This is what wrong submission is.

Jesus said quite clearly, *"If any one comes to me and does not hate his own father and mother and wife and children and brothers and sisters, yes, and even his own life, he cannot be my disciple"* (Luke 14:26). Does this mean that we hate them, that we reject them? Surely not, but rather it is the will of God in our lives concerning our families which comes before the will of the family member. If there is wrong doing, this must be pointed out. If attitudes or behaviour is wrong, this must be pointed out. If there is sin, this must be addressed. Whatever it is, if this is going against the fundamental will of God, that is, the commandments, we are to speak up. If our children want to do something that we know is not of God, then what do we do?

Do we pat them on the back and say, 'Well done' so as not to hurt their feelings? No, it is our duty to tell them it is not of God, then leave it in God's hands. If my husband or wife is going to make a decision that would mean going against God's will or commandment, then it is up to me to point this out to him or her, then leave it in God's hands.

We have, in our lives, many a time, suffered in wrong relationships, be it a broken or wounded marriage, suffering through parents, a father or mother, siblings, friendships, etc. Let us touch on a couple of areas where these situations have affected our lives, our own attitudes and reactions as we allow the Lord to enter into our hearts and minds and heal the wounds and where necessary even repent of any wrong doing we may have done. We will see how we have been affected into wrong submission and how the Lord wants us to stand straight and to look up to Him.

False submission

False submission is primarily caused through oppressive authority be it government, office, society, home, friends, or sadly even certain persons in the church. When a person oppresses another either through physical, emotional, psychological, or sexual violence through domination, that person becomes frightened and can retreat into a demeaning frame and thought patterns that lead to false submission. Unless the person is very strong and can stand up to the oppression, then false submission is inevitable.

Misogyny

A very common attitude and means of false submission is the **misogynistic** attitude, which is not only ungodly but very sinful in the eyes of God and Christian living. Misogyny is fundamentally the hatred of woman and all that she represents. A misogynist, or one with misogynistic traits, is more often a man; however, women can be misogynists but that then turns into another situation altogether. It has been interesting to note that a patriarchal society can easily be a means of hiding for the misogynist. A misogynist cannot bear a woman's creative and intuitive being. She would not be able to have her own mind, an opinion, or think for herself. Education or study is very often scorned at and she is reduced to menial work. He will not tolerate her capacity to be gifted or the notion that she is capable of living outside of serving and living for him. That she can live independently as a person is simply not acceptable to a misogynist. Man can be controlling in his attitude to woman and then towards the children. She becomes a virtual slave to his needs and wants. This kind of behaviour would inevitably lead to the breakdown of marriage since the misogynist has no notion of the true meaning of marriage. In these cases, children are left without a father both in the case if the father is domineering and controlling, since that destroys the very essence of fatherhood which is a caring, providing, and protecting role.

• A lot of the time behind this hatred for woman lies either a broken and wrong relationship with the mother.

• A deep-seated bitterness, resentment, and anger towards a female which is now projected to women in general. This attitude would then lead to the inability to bond well with any woman let alone the wife or female partner or companion.

• A man would have had his own father, or male members of his family, friends, peers acting in this manner. That person was his dysfunctional role model.

• Another type of misogyny is when the female members of the family including daughters are completely ignored as non-existent. The fathers run after and uphold the son, whereas the daughters are ignored as they cannot and are not expected to be anywhere near as intelligent as the men, therefore, why bother with them. The father would give them a basic education but we would not expect much from them. This kind of misogyny can also be seen in mothers. The son is everything and the daughters are just extensions of the furniture. Much more can be said in this area.

- Then there is a misogyny as that in various cultures where there is a total devaluation of the female and their rights as persons including their education or giftedness. The woman is treated as an object and slave without any form or say in her life.

- The result and effects of misogyny is pronounced: fear, depression, stress, a deep self-hatred which can often lead to suicide and a rage or even hatred towards men which is *misan•ry*.

Misogyny and *misan•ry* often lead to the rejection of the woman's femininity which could then turn to same gender issues or extreme feminist attitudes. Misogyny can also be seen in the generational attitudes of men where the son becomes and acts towards his wife or sisters as the father did towards the mother and daughters. There are times when women would feel within their deepest being the hatred of the misogynistic men in their generational tree and would need healing from the misogyny coming down through the generations.

Healing

When the woman's centre of being has been destroyed, it needs healing. The woman would have a very weak or suppressed sense of identity and can only see herself in and through the eyes of all the lies that she has been told about herself. Deep healing is needed and the Lord comes in to renew and strengthen her centre. Mary, Our Lady, is very prominent in this type of healing for she is the complete woman and she comes to hold her child, leading women to safety. Many a time St. Joseph has been the man to come and stand by the woman. He who was the righteous husband of Mary and treated her with so much love and respect comes to help and nurture the women with Mary.

Misandry

Misan*ry is the hatred, fear, and contempt for men, as well as a hatred towards one's own true femininity, a trait that is a pronounced feminist movement.

Let us now see how *misogyny* and *misan*ry* are related but must also be separated.

> First, we must acknowledge that misandry is partly reality-based to the extent that it is in part a reaction to misogyny, and to the real or perceived oppression of women by men. Misogyny generates misandry. The truth is if you throw a boomerang it will hit you back.

> Misandry is often grounded, like misogyny, in nasty personal experiences. Many women could say that they have had unkind and even spiteful personal experiences with men: fathers, brothers, lovers, co-workers, bosses. However, this does not mean that this results in an attitude of misandry. The truth is, we have all been hurt by members of the opposite sex, and by members of our own sex as well. So we cannot generalise.

> A deep anger, resentment, and bitterness toward a male member of the family, male friends or peers could reflect isolated traits of misandry. However, if this is not identified, it could and would, in turn, be projected onto men in general. Unless healed this could evolve into a real attitude of misandry.

> The very sad situation is that like a misogynist, a misandrist, a woman will use men for her own ends to get back at them. She would feel justified in this way. This is totally wrong.

> In the misanderous woman, there is the open wound for the spirit of Jezebel to enter and to wreck havoc not only upon the woman herself but to all those around her.

If we find ourselves in this scenario it is very important that we turn to Jesus. We forgive those who hurt us and repent of our own attitudes, for both are necessary; healing is very necessary. However, having said the above, what are we saying? What is the relationship between the man and the woman? When are we and when are we not to be submissive? Now one thing must be made clear: to be submissive does not mean to be subservient.

True submission

Submission or surrender is in itself a feminine trait. We have said that we are all feminine unto God. In each person, both men and women, we have within us both the male and female traits, the anima and animus, then depending upon our gender that trait is uppermost; that is, the man would have the animus trait uppermost whereas the female would have the anima uppermost. To place everything in the right context, BOTH MAN AND WOMAN reach their fulfilment as persons in their identity, roles, work, activity, etc. They are complimentary yet different, for both are called by God to be submissive one to the other. To be a person means to strive towards self-realisation and this can only be achieved through the gift of self, each in their own giftedness and qualities. This is true submission. When the self has been taken by force or oppressed, where it has been destroyed then there cannot be a realisation that comes from God. It is not from God, for the Lord gives freely and wants us to reach that realisation of self in and through Him and through the love of one another.

Man and woman are meant to live in holy submission one to the other. The Gospel of Christ speaks to us of the dignity and rational freedom of the man and woman capable of knowing and loving God. They are invited to live in a communion of love and are called to mirror that love that is in God. It is a question of mutual relationship in a way that both the man and the woman are to reach the apex of their capabilities, the giftedness given to each one, in and through each other. Each one is to encourage and give freedom to the other to grow and to become.

The biblical and evangelical truth speaks about the *'unity of the two.'* The truth is, both men and women are to be submissive to each other in Christ in their originality and diversity as in Ephesians 2:14: *"the wall of hostility has been broken ⲟown in Christ."* As we have already mentioned, because of the abuse of their true dignity, both men and women have lost sight of who they truly are and so cannot reach the fulfilment God has intended for them.

A text on true submission that has been so abused is Ephesians 5:21-33. Wives be subject to your husband, etc., but also husbands love your wives as Christ loves the Church. Now how did Christ love the Church? Christ washed the disciples' feet. He died for the church and gave all He had for her. In turn, the wife loves the husband seeing such love coming from him. This is a love that flows one to the other through Christ.

"For true love is inexhaustible; the more you give, the more you have. An⬧ if you go to ⬧raw at the true fountainhea⬧, the more water you ⬧raw, the more abun⬧ant is its flow" (Antoine de Saint-Exupéry).

To submit oneself, to surrender oneself is not a destruction of the self. We do not lose anything of ourselves, but we gain and become who we truly are and are meant to be, even with friends, with colleagues at work, with those entrusted in your care or under you at work. Respect, care, encourage, and protect the dignity of those who work with or for us. These are all means of love that reflect the love of Christ. It is in dying that we find our life and true worth.Love is both man and woman looking up towards God and receiving from Him in a way that both man and woman might serve each other in love and in fulfilment of the purposes laid out by

God. But we have to understand the true meaning of submission or surrender and reject that which is false, that which makes us bent. Submission means to surrender; it means to serve. We know that meekness is not weakness, yet both these aspects have been so misunderstood and misused.

When we learn to live from the centre in Christ, we find fullness of being; we find true submission and can enter into fruitful obedience to God the Father. Mary responded to the words of the angel; she responded in full surrender. Mary was called to be the mother of Jesus, yet she allowed Joseph to lead her. They talked, discussed, and prayed. As Jesus grew, He learned from them the essence of love until He Himself became aware of being "the Servant of the Lord and Son of God."

Obedience is serving

As the people of God, we are to hear God's Word and to respond to it. Mary is the arch-type, the second Eve of the personal dignity of women. She listens, absorbs and responds; she surrenders and submits. Her surrendering, her submission to the Word of God given to her by the angel was not a subservient action, but one of obedience knowing who is calling and speaking to her. In her expression *"han•mai• of the Lor•"* (Luke 1:38), Mary knew her place before God as creature. It is in serving that we become. To serve both like Jesus and

Mary is to be under obedience to God, for Jesus said in John 4:34, "*My foo• is to •o the will of him who sent me, an• to accomplish his work.*" Mary said in Luke 1:38, "*Behol•, I am the han•mai• of the Lor•; let it be to me accor•ing to your wor•.*" Both Jesus and Mary placed themselves in the service of God the Father, in the service of His love and will for the sake of mankind. Had Mary not said '*Yes*,' the plan of salvation would not have been fulfilled. When we place ourselves in the service of others, we are walking in obedience to the Word given to us in Christ. Mary walks with us. In her serving, she ran to her cousin Elisabeth to care for her in her last trimester of her pregnancy. "*Whoever wants to be first must be last of all an• servant of all*" we are told in Mark 9:35.

The dignity of every person, our vocation and depth of being finds its ultimate in union with God. Mary is the most complete expression of this dignity and vocation. No human being, man or woman, created in the image and likeness of God can in any way attain fulfilment apart from this image and likeness. For we have come from God and must go back to God. It is in our complete surrender and obedience that we truly discover and attain who we are in Christ and become fulfilled women and men of God.

chapter fifteen
the healing of the family tree (intergenerational healing)

We may not have thought of it, but we form part of a great work of God, the family tree. The Lord has placed us in time and space in our family. We live in the here and now to understand what the Lord wants of us and how we can be instruments in the Lord's hands for the healing of our family tree or intergenerational healing and pour out blessings to our future generations.

We all have our freedom and uniqueness from and in God. The Lord will never touch that for it is our own identity.

However, this identity, our character, our behaviour, temperament, part of it at least depends on the family tree to which we belong. We have our ancestors who go down the line from generation to generation. These ancestors have given us both the positive and the negative attitudes which we have inherited. We have either inherited them directly or have a disposition to inherit. No one is perfect. It is interesting, for if we look at Jesus' genealogy found in Matthew 1:1-17, we will see a lot of names, many of which may not mean anything to us. What is the purpose of this genealogy? In reality, this genealogy is interesting for neither was Jesus' family tree perfect. We will find that in His family tree were prostitutes (Rahab), murderers, adulterers (David). So, we can imagine what there can be in our own family tree. We all have a family tree wherein there is the positive and the negative.

Sometimes there can be many misunderstandings and confusion regarding the healing of the family tree.

Why is this? In chapter 4 of Exodus, it is written that the sin of our ancestors will pass to the 3rd and 4th generation. But then in Ezekiel chapter 18, it says that every person is responsible for their own sins. The father is not responsible for the son's sins and neither is the son responsible for the sins of the father. Some maintain the text of Exodus is saying that we inherit the actual sin, but this is not the case. Unless the sin is repented of and brought to the Cross of Christ, we do reap the effects of the past sins. We are adversely affected by the sins of parents, grandparents, great-grandparents, and by the sins of the ancestors who adversely affected them. There may even be some group or church leaders who uphold that we inherit the actual sin. We do not inherit any sin, that is, the actual guilt of the sin at all. We only inherit original sin, but we are all responsible for our own sin.

When we talk of the healing of the family tree, we are not talking about inheriting the sin of the family but the disposition to that particular sin. If a grandfather was aggressive, then the father was aggressive, there is a very good chance of the son being aggressive or being disposed to aggression, the effects and wound of the sin of aggression is in the family line. Let me explain. If we go to the doctor with a chest pain, he asks us about our family whether there is a heart problem in our father or mother. We answer him "I came for myself, not for my father or mother". He will agree but he needs this information. He is looking for the disposition to heart problems, diabetes, high blood pressure. Why? If a parent had this sickness, the weakness, the chances of this happening is in the family line. We all accept this medically.

We can have a disposition to a certain sickness if it is in the family.

From the psychological aspect it is the same. We would sometimes find a fine line of depression where the grandfather had depression, the uncle and aunt as well. This does not mean that I will struggle with depression, but I will be aware that once it is there in the family tree, then it would be easy for me to have a disposition to it. We would see even in the behaviour patterns of family, where there would be timidity or aggression, alcoholism, etc. So there will be the tendency to this psychological weakness. We, however, admit that we can have tendencies to certain sins rather than to others. For example: If we have in our family tree the recurrent sin of adultery which turns out to be a common sin in the family, it could be then that if one had a problem in one's marriage, the first thought, to fill the pain or gap would be to find someone outside the marriage, and thus risk committing the sin of adultery. This is because the disposition is greater in you than, perhaps, someone else, as it is very common in your family tree.

In some families, there is a recurrent pattern of broken families in the family tree. If this is the case, the chance of wanting to break up a marriage if there is a problem would be greater. One would then have to be careful and on one's guard. There is a disposition to this. This happens even if one does not know of the ancestral situations. Take for example suicide. This can come when there are massive problems which people try to solve with drugs, gambling, alcohol, pornography, etc. This then brings in a disposition to suicide. So, one would be inheriting the disposition, not the sin.

It could be that the whole family is in a situation of adultery, but if you are not doing this then you are not responsible for the family's sin. If we are in an office where everyone smokes, but I do not smoke, going to the office, day after day, into that environment will eventually affect me without me knowing it. In fact, doctors call it passive smoking. It is in this respect that we can talk of the healing of the family tree. We do not inherit the actual sins, but only the disposition; the environment is affecting me which is not allowing me to live my life in freedom. Our environment, our surroundings, our family, our family tree affect us. If there is unforgiveness in the family, deep grudges, family and neighbourhood quarrels, etc., this creates a very deep platform for negativity to pass through to future generations. All must be forgiven and brought to the Cross of Christ.

When we look at our own genealogy, which many of us do not remember or even know save for the last couple of generations, it could be that in my family tree there could be murderers, or people who were murdered. There could be criminals. It could be that there were persons involved in the occult or Freemasonry or involved in spiritism or Satanism. Some could have been anticlerical or against God, unbelievers. These would have left a trail of negativity down the line.

Having said that we must also say that we do not only inherit the negative, but we also inherit the positive, that which is holy. If our grandmother was a holy woman, praying continuously then we are also inheriting from her. We are inheriting blessings from our grandmother. So, we are not only inheriting the negative but also the positive. No family tree is perfect, not even that of Jesus. We also inherit the blessings which our ancestors have left us. We can thank God and our family for the benefit from our virtuous ancestors going back a thousand generations (Sir 44:10-12).

One of the most dangerous aspects in the family tree is the curse, one that is verbal, especially that of the father or mother on the children. The strongest ones are those of the parents and the spiritual director/leader. Why? The parents have a legal authority on their children. So, when a parent curses their child verbally it causes tremendous damage emotionally and psychologically. Any curse a parent could do, especially through any form of ritual is very bad, indeed. The parent is opening the door to the evil one who then has a legal right on that child because the parent has a legal right and has placed that child in the way of the evil one. In the same way, the spiritual director/leader who curses his directee/church attendee, opens the door to the evil one.

Unfortunately, there are parents who curse their children even in their everyday speech. One may not mean it, so it is important to watch our words for they have effect. If a parent is constantly speaking negatively about or to their children, this brings about a devastating effect. There may be ignorance behind this, but we need to learn and know its negative impact. Then, there are some parents who do not bless the marriage of their children because they do not approve of the marriage. So, without the blessing they curse them. There are those parents who curse the womb because they reject the marriage. If a mother is pregnant and does not want the child, she does not curse the child but would wish it to be miscarried, but does not; this can cause eventual miscarriages and abortions in the family line.

So, these curses go down from generation to generation. We pray and break the curses. We are here speaking about the dispositions and the problems that could occur in the family tree.

Let us say that your father or mother left you a house in their will, what would you do? Take the house and go in and clean it. If your father was a collector of daily newspapers and magazines, out of respect to your father, would you keep that hoard of paper? No. You respect and love your father. You would keep the house, but you would clear it of all the newspapers and magazines. It is not a lack of respect to clear the family tree from any rubbish that may be in this house. We are asking the Lord to bless all that is good and holy but to break and remove all that is not good and is negative. We are cleaning up the inheritance that has been left to us, for we want to proclaim into our family line that which Joshua said in Joshua 24:15 of his house: *"for me an* my house, we will serve the LORD."* We not only have the right to do it, but should do it. We keep what is good and discard all that is not holy. The Lord has placed us here in this moment in time for this very purpose.

Let us speak about ancestral memory. What is this?

This happens when a person is going through very intense healing. We all hold memories in our subconscious and as you may or may not know, memory can also be very selective. Often something may have happened in our family which we may have completely forgotten. Or there is a story that your parents or grandparents or even great grandparents had told you, something that happened years before in the family and you thought nothing of it. Or a story that was passed down of what happened a very long time ago, even generations ago. Suddenly, this memory is brought to mind and you see that in your situation; this all begins to fit into a pattern.

Ancestral memory is also passed down the line when there has been strong trauma. The effects of trauma and negativity can pass on to generations if it is not cut and brought to the Cross of Christ. There was a case of a girl who suffered an extreme form of claustrophobia because she was locked up by her friends as a joke. In the same way her mother had suffered being locked and closed up and so had her grandmother. They all had different experiences but the effect of the trauma was the same. With the subconscious memory going back generations we may see and begin to understand the roots of our problem when these memories are brought to the surface. Sometimes the memory may go back generations. We pray and bring in the Blood and Cross of Christ into this situation to set us free.

As a nation we have collective and historical memories which would also need healing. What has happened in our nation? What of our people? We have things of the past whose memory has been kept alive so that we might pray for the healing.

For example: After the wars or traumatic situations in a country, there may be a Memorial wherein once a year the government would place wreaths under the Memorial *'lest we forget.'* We need to pray for these and go through our country's generational healing.

One active way of remembering is through the practice of rituals. The Jewish Passover Seder, the ritual meal with a liturgy that celebrates Jewish freedom from slavery in Egypt, is perhaps one of the best examples of the actualization of memory. The entire Seder can in some sense be seen as a symbolic reenactment of a historical moment. Moreover, one of the central dictums of the Seder, *"in each and every generation let each person regard him- or herself as though they had emerged from Egypt,"* enforces the fusion of past and present.

Then the very true healing is the Consecration of Eucharist wherein we bring to present the Cross and Resurrection of Jesus that we may all be healed.

God who is the great "I AM" is not bound by time, but is outside time. For Him there is no past, no future only the present. So, when we pray, we are bringing all things into the present to Him to heal, deliver, and set free.

It is good to leave those who come after us some material inheritance, but there is the other spiritual inheritance that is at stake. Are we leaving our children values? Faith? This is important for in the future we do not know how this will affect them. We do not wish to leave anything negative behind us. We want to leave all that is positive, good, and holy. We want to bless our children and our children's children. The blessings of parents are priceless. When the Lord gave us children, He gave us a mission. Children are not ours but His for us to care for. Even if there are couples without children, the blessings the husband gives to the wife and the wife to the husband are very significant. Blessings are very important and are worth their weight in gold. Then there are the blessings that the children give to the parents. Parents and children should pray for each other. These are the greatest blessings that a family can give to each other. The blessing of a mother is vital to the husband and children as is that of the father to the wife and children. This blessing would also form an inheritance of blessings to the coming generations. Bless also your neighbours and the people you meet.

There is the question of why this evil. Why does the Lord allow this evil? It is about the freedom of will. We can argue that it is not fair for the children to suffer the consequences of the evil of the previous generations. Ezekiel 18:2 says, *"The parents eat sour grapes, and the children's teeth are set on edge."*

This is why we have prayer and we have the Lord. This is the result of sin. We have been given free will to do good or to do evil. We can repent of our sin and convert to do good. God did not create robots. If God prevented and stopped everyone from doing evil, then He would be removing our free will and true love would not exist, for love would be mandatory. It would not be a choice and that is not love. It is not freedom to love or not to love. We ask the Lord to help us. If God were to remove all evil He would be removing all our liberty and freedom, and instead of being children of the Father we would be robots which it not His intention. The Lord wants us to love out of our own free will.

How do we pray for the healing of the family tree?

- We pray as the Lord shows us for all those situations in our lives and family that need healing.

- We may have physical health needs, emotional needs, spiritual needs, and interpersonal needs. Have many of my problems been caused by my own failures, neglect, and sinfulness?

- We pray to the Lord to forgive. We humbly ask the Lord to forgive the sins of our ancestors whose failures have left their effects on us in the form of unwanted tendencies, behaviour patterns, and weaknesses in body, mind, and spirit. We ask the Lord to heal any hereditary illness and disorders.

- We forgive those who have gone before us. If our ancestors have sinned we are not to judge for we cannot say what happened. What we do know is that we are suffering the consequences of the situations.

- We ask the Lord to deliver us and our entire family tree from the influence of the evil one, to free all living and dead members of our family tree from any effects of unrepented sin, pacts, satanism, occult that any member of our family may have dabbled with. We include those of our family members who are in adoptive relationships and include the extended families that come through marriage. We ask the Lord to forgive and release us from any contaminating form of bondage.

- We stand here present in time as a living member of the family tree, and we pray to the Lord for their forgiveness and we forgive them. If we do not forgive then our prayer is blocked. The Lord wants to forgive, but we, here standing before the Lord, have to open these doors. At this point we can pray Baruch ch 3:1-14.

- If there are any curses, we pray for them to be turned into blessings. If the marriages are cursed then we pray for it to be turned into a blessing. We pray to break any curse on the womb and to give fertility.

- We pray for the breaking of all negative effects coming down through the past generations of the family line and to prevent them from continuing onto the future generations.

- We also offer a Mass for the intention of our ancestors and the cleansing of the family tree (Mass of the Blood of Jesus).

- We symbolically place the Cross of Jesus Christ over the head of each person in the family tree and between each generation. We place the Cross facing the previous generations to heal and to restore. We place the Cross facing all future generations that they may be blessed. We ask the Lord to let the cleansing blood of Jesus purify the blood lines in our family lineage.

- We pray to break any form of tie or link that we may have. If we have any dispositions, be it spiritual, psychological, or physical, that is alcohol, aggression, pornography, etc., we pray to the Lord to break this bondage and to bring freedom.

- In our family tree, we replace all bondage with a holy bonding in family love for there to be a deep bonding with the Lord Jesus Christ in the power of the Holy Spirit. We pray for the Holy Trinity to pervade the whole family tree with love and unity so that the whole family may recognise and manifest this love in their relationships and lives. We also include all those needs which are still unknown to us but known to the Lord.

- We bless our children, our families, husbands, wives and all future generations and place them into the hands and heart of the Lord that He would bless and give them life in HIM.

Romans 8:17 tells us *"But if we are chil*ren, we are heirs as well: heirs of Go*, heirs with Christ."* Through this breaking and healing of the negative bonds in the family line, we are cleansing not only the past generations but laying new foundations for the future generations. We bring everything under Christ so that those who have gone before us may enter into the Kingdom as true children and heirs of God (Acts 10:40). We do this by not only sharing in the death and resurrection of Jesus through baptism, healing prayer, the Healing Mass, but by living in true faith in Jesus as Lord. *"This means that if anyone is in Christ, he is a new creation. The ol• or•er has passe• away; now all is new"* (2 Corinthians 5:17).

Truly the old order has passed away and the new creation has come. This is not only for us, but for our families. The blessings of the new generations will unfold wherein we pass on the promises of the Lord to those coming after us. *"Praise the LORD. Blesse• is the man who fears the LORD, who greatly •elights in his comman•ments! His •escen•ants will be mighty in the lan•; the generations of the upright will be blesse•"* (Psalm 112:2).

chapter sixteen
the commandment to love

The first commandment is to love God with all our being and the second is to love our neighbour as ourselves. This is what the Lord wants of us. If we are to love others and we cannot love ourselves aright, then how are we to love our neighbour the way the Father wants us to love them, wholly and truthfully? The way we love others is to be in like manner as the Father loves us, for He told us *"Love one another as I have love• you!"*

There are three commandments that are important here:

1. To love God with all our heart, mind and soul
2. To love ourselves

3. To love our neighbour as ourselves

Self-love in the true Christian way is the proper foundation for the love of others. We do not mean egoism or narcissism, but true Christian self-love. We cannot love others properly if we are still living out of our broken and unhealed self. The child within will always be wanting attention, for our love is then a needy love and not free and giving. When we are unhealed then the child within will always be crying out for attention in one way or another, and these expressions can be very subtle. This does not mean that we do not love, but the more we are healed the more we are able to love others as Christ wants us to. God's love for us is unconditional; it makes us whole. He knows about our sin, but what He cares for most is that we turn to Him. What He wants is that we receive His love.

Our true self-love comes when we receive and allow the Lord to love us, when His unconditional love touches our deepest being and begins to make us whole. We truly come home when God the Father touches us at our deepest level and we enter into a relationship with Him. We no longer feel like orphans but are truly wanted and have that strong sense of belonging. We often talk of the Prodigal son. The father did not care that the son was dirty; he just hugged him, and that is what the Father does to us: He just wants us home.

Sometimes, when we are still unhealed, we change Jesus' words from 'Love your neighbour as yourself to '*love your neighbour an• hate yourself, humiliate yourself, •owngra•e yourself, etc.*' This is all a lie. We think that God the Father wants us to dislike ourselves for us to be humble, but this is not humility at all. Did Jesus dislike Himself? Did Mary dislike herself? Yet they were truly the humble ones. We need to re-understand these things. They were living in the truth of their identity. There was no problem there. They died to self, to their own ideas and plans so that they would be obedient to the Father.

Healthy self-esteem and self-love

Good and healthy self-esteem is important for any relationship, especially between parents and children, husband and wife. Husbands, if you do not have a healthy self-worth of yourselves you cannot love your wives properly.

"*With all humility an• gentleness, with patience, bearing with one another in love, eager to maintain the unity of the Spirit in the bon• of peace*" (Ephesians 4:23).

If you have been belittled, have lack of self-worth, low self-esteem, etc., and you are still unhealed you will very likely do the same to your spouse and treat your spouse in a very abusive way. To love ourselves is to love our family. We also need good and balanced self-esteem to be good neighbours and friends. We are not to debase ourselves thinking this is humility, which it is not. Nor are we to think too highly of ourselves our abilities, gifts, and talents, but we are to be of good judgment.

Paul tells us in Romans 12:3, "*For by the grace given to me I say to everyone you are not to think of yourself more highly that you ought to think, but to think with sober ju*gment*"*. Paul keeps us in check. We are not to have pride and arrogance that oppresses others. Nothing destroys relationships more than pride. We are to have that healthy balance of approach to ourselves which is the truth. That is true humility. We are to trust God. We are to be humble before the Lord for He knows our inner hearts. We are to know our strengths and weaknesses and smile at them. True humility is truth and trust in God.

Self-worth

It is the Lord who tells us who we are. It is He who gives us identity and self-worth, not our husband or wife, colleagues or friends. We have to be careful that our self-worth is not dependent on others for we would then become bent to them and open to being wounded. We are not to look to people for constant permission to be, to live, and to function. We live because we are children of God, and this is a gift that is given to us from the Father. No one can take it from us for it is ours and is intrinsic to our identity. We know we are the temple of the Lord and as such are being built and strengthened. It may be damaged and we may not be aware of it, but it cannot be taken from us unless we decide to give it away.

No one in their right mind would willingly give away their passport or identity to someone else, so then, why should we give away our identity in Christ? Our identity in Christ is who we are. That is why our healing is important. Our image and the image of God is important for it affects our identity as children of the Father. We are to mirror the true image of God which is reflected in Christ who is the Imago Dei, that is, the true Image of God the Father. The inner child within yearns for God and the truth. If we had to ask the question, *'Di* Go* give you the right to hurt a chil* He loves?'* you will surely answer *'No. Of course not!'* Then what right do any of us have to reject and belittle ourselves, we who are His children. Who gave you the right to throw yourself away in sin? Who gave you the right to call yourself rubbish? God delights in us, in each and every one of us, in you and in me.

Jesus the Imago Dei

We need to work with this and to co-operate with the Holy Spirit so that the re-wiring of our hearts and minds will bring forth the fruit it is meant to. Our identity is then not formed by those distorted mirror images but by the true image and mirror that is Jesus Christ. He is the Incarnate one, the true image of the Father – the Imago Dei of the Father. In Colossians, Paul tells us that we are made in the image of Jesus. Jesus told us, told Philip in the Gospel of John *"Who has seen me has seen the Father, for I an♦ the Father are One."* If Jesus reflects and is the true image of the Father and we are made in the image of Jesus who is the Incarnate one, we are made in the image of God. That is how precious we are. Christ affirms us, the Father affirms us, and the Spirit affirms us. He has given us everything. Jesus existed before time. He existed before He was born of Mary and came into the world. These are deep mysteries, but we know that God created man and woman in His image and likeness and placed them upon the earth breathing His Spirit and life into them. Jesus is faithful and true and will not fail us for He is love. St. Paul says in 1 Corinthians 13, in the beautiful eulogy of love, *"all things will come to an en♦ but love will remain."* This is how precious we are to the Father. Each and every person who has ever been conceived and lived in this world belongs to Him and are made for His glory.

When we allow God to love us, we change. The child within us changes and we are made whole. God affirms us and shows us how we are to love ourselves and love others. He can and does do it for He is faithful and true to His Word.

Prayer

Lord, we thank You for what You do for and with us. We count it a blessing that each one of us are made in Your image and likeness. As You heal the child in us, Lord, You will bring us to full identity in You and restore our image in You.

Printed in Great Britain
by Amazon